"Islamic Worship Reference" series *1*

Fundamentals of
Islam

Imam Muhammad Shirazi

fountain books

BM Box 8545
London WC1N 3XX
UK
www.fountainbooks.co.uk

In association with
Free Muslim
PO Box 13/5570
Beirut, Lebanon
www.freemuslim.org

First published 2001

© *fountain books*

British Library Cataloguing in Publication Data.

A catalogue record for this book is available from the British Library.

ISBN   1-903323-06-1

Cover design by Ali Saleh

In the Name of Allah, The Beneficent The Merciful.
All Praise is to Him, Lord of the Worlds.
Let Allah's Blessings be upon Muhammad
and upon his righteous and pure family.

Fundamentals of Islam

Table of Contents

Editor's Foreword

Islam is a unique and indivisible system that provides a complete and comprehensive set of teachings, addressing the issues of concern to both life of this world and that of the hereafter.

In this brief discourse the author outlines the five axioms of Islam (*Usul el Deen*), which are the Oneness of God, Divine Justice, Prophethood, *Imamah* (leadership of mankind) and Resurrection.

In addressing the role and significance of the holy Qur'an, the author then presents various *hadiths* narrated from the Messenger of Allah, Muhammad (S)[1], and the infallible Imams (A)[2].

In the third section of this work, the author presents a question and answer dialogue on the Islamic system of government, discussing such a system from the various domains of politics, economics, the army, freedom, peace, judicial system, health, education, family. Through this discussion the author establishes that a government based on the teachings of Islam would provide the most favourable system of government for mankind.

In the final part of this work, the author lists some of the *haram* (forbidden) actions or conducts an individual may come across in everyday affairs. Also included separately are lists of the 'detestable' and the 'ethically desirable conducts.

Z. Olyabek
London
February 2001

---

[1] *Sall-Allah Alayhi wa Aalihi wa Sallam,* meaning Peace and Blessings of Allah be upon him and his infallible family. This invocation is always made after the mention of the name of the Messenger of Allah out of respect and devotion for the last messenger of Allah, Muhammad (S).

[2] *Alayhum as-Salaam (plural) or Alayh as-Salaam (singular),* meaning peace be upon them or him/her. This invocation is always made after the mention of the name of a prophet or infallible Imam / person (A).

Fundamentals of Islam

Fundamental Principles

The fundamental principles of Islam (*Usul el Deen*), which are the 'pillars' of Islam, are five. A Muslim must believe in all five principles; no more and no less. The five fundamental principles are:

1. The Oneness (*Tawheed*) of the Supreme Being and Creator of All Things.
2. Justice of the Supreme Being. (*'Adl*)
3. The Prophethood. (*Nobuwwah*)
4. The Leadership of Mankind. (*Imamah*)
5. The Resurrection. (*Me'ad*)

1. The Indivisible Oneness of God

Tawheed is the belief that the universe and all existence has a deity who created them all, and brought everything into existence from nihility and that he sustains and maintains everything. Therefore creation, sustenance, bestowing, denying, death, life, sickness, health, etc. are all under His control and will . . .

"His command is indeed such that if He wills a thing, He says to it "Be", and it becomes to be" - The holy Qur'an; YaSeen (36): 82.

The evidence for existence of Allah Almighty is what we see around us. The sky and whatever there is in it; the sun, the moon, and all other stars and galaxies. The clouds, the winds, the rain . . . and the earth and whatever in it such as the seas and rivers, the trees and the fruits, the various kinds of precious mines such as gold, silver, and emerald mines. As well as the various categories of animals; those that fly, and those who live in water or on land, having a variety of shapes, sizes, and sounds. And then there is this wonderful human being who has various sensory powers, feelings, and abilities.

All of these are evidence of the existence of an All-wise and omniscient.

Creator in Whom we believe and Whom we worship, from Whom we ask help and in Whom we trust.

Allah, the Most High has many attributes:

He is omniscient, He knows about all things big and small. He knows what people may have in their hearts.

He is Almighty all things are in His control.

He has the power to create things, give them sustenance, and let them die or give them life.

He is forever living and never dies.

He wills things that are useful and He does not will things that are not useful.

He sees all things, He hears the voice of all things even if it would only be a whisper.

His existence is from eternity to eternity.

He created things when nothing existed. He will live when nothing will exist.

He speaks to any of His sincere servants whom He wills; like His messengers, and the angels.

He is truthful and never disregards His promise.

He is the Creator, the provider, the life giver, the source of bounties with the power to stop them also; He is merciful, forgiving, Majestic Honourable and Generous.

Allah, the Most High is free of all shortcomings:

He does not have a body like ours. He is not composed of parts and He can never be seen in this world or in the hereafter. He is not subject to affects, changes, or development. He does not feel hungry and He never gets old. He has no partner or companion and He is the only One Supreme Being.

His attributes are not different from His essence.

Thus, He is Omniscient and Almighty since eternity, not like us who were ignorant at a time and then acquired knowledge or were weak at a time and then became strong.

He is self-sufficient. He does not need any consultations or helper or secretaries or any army to protect His person etc.

2. Divine Justice

Divine justice means that Allah does not do any injustice to anyone and does not do anything that would be against wisdom. Therefore, whatever He has created, or whatever amount of sustenance He has given to someone or whatever He has not given to someone all are on the basis of wisdom and on good grounds even though we do not know the reasons. It is simply like a physician prescribing a certain medicine for a patient that we consider is good and useful even though we may not know all the evidence for its usefulness.

If we see that Allah has granted someone wealth and He did not do so for someone else, or He caused someone to become sick and has kept another person healthy, etc. in all such cases we must believe that all of such cases are based on Allah's knowledge and wisdom even though we may not be aware of the wisdom of such decisions.

It is stated in some *Hadith*, or traditions, that Moses (A) asked Allah to let him know something about His Justice, which would not be a clear example of justice. Allah ordered him to go to a certain water fountain in the wilderness to see certain things that would take place therein. When Moses (A) arrived at the fountain, he saw a horseman who had arrived at the fountain to freshen up. When the horseman left the scene, he left a bag of money behind. Afterwards, a child came to the fountain, saw and picked up the bag of money and left. Then a blind man came to the fountain to wash himself for prayer, and at this time the horseman came back and accused the blind man of taking the bag of money he had left behind. As a result a dispute flared up between the horseman and the blind man, and subsequently the horseman killed the blind man.

Allah then revealed to Moses (A) that the horseman had stolen the bag of money from the father of the child (who came to pick up the bag of money left behind at the fountain by the horseman.) In this way the property was returned to the rightful owner. The blind man had previously killed the father of the horseman and therefore the horseman at the end punished the killer of his father.

This is how Allah's justice and wisdom works, even though it may look some how far from the conventional rules.

3. Prophethood

A prophet is the person who receives divine revelations. The prophets are of two kinds of status:

(1) The *Mursal* Prophets

They were those prophets who were commissioned to guide people out of darkness to light, out of falsehood to the truth, from myths and superstition to reality and out of ignorance to knowledge.

(2) The non-*Mursal* Prophets.

They were those prophets who just received divine revelations for themselves only and they had not received orders to preach such revelations to people.

In total there were one hundred and twenty four thousand prophets but the *Mursal* prophets among them were just a few.

The first of the prophets was Prophet Adam (A) and the last of them was Prophet Muhammad (S).

The *Mursal* prophets are in two categories:

A. The *Ulul-Azm* prophets; who are universal prophets who had received divine orders to preach to and lead the whole of mankind. They were:

    i.   Abraham (*Ibrahim*),
    ii.   Noah, (*Nuh*)
    iii. Moses, (*Mussa*)
    iv. Jesus (*'Essa*)
    v.   Muhammad, peace be upon them all.

Jews are followers of Moses, (A), Christians are followers of Jesus, (A) and Muslims are followers of Muhammad (S) and his infallible family.

B. The non-*Ulul-Azm* prophets are those who have been sent to preach to their nations only.

However, Islam abrogated and superseded all the previous religions, and therefore one may not persist on them but it is imperative upon all to follow the Teachings of Islam, as Allah Almighty says:

"Whoever seeks a religion other than Islam, it will never be accepted from him, and in the Hereafter he will be one of the losers." - The holy Qur'an; The Family of 'Emran (3): 85.

Therefore Judaism and Christianity are false and Islam remains the Law of Allah until the Day of Judgment and will never be superseded.

Therefore, Prophet Muhammad (S) is the last of the prophets and the religion revealed to him, Islam, nullifies other religions and supersede them all and that his law remains effective and valid until the Day of Judgment.

A Brief Biography of Prophet Muhammad (S)

He is Muhammad the son of Abdullah and *Aminah bint Wahab*. He was born at dawn on Friday, the seventeenth of *Rabi'-I* in the year of the Elephant in Mecca during the time of *Casra,* the 'Just' king of Persia. He received Divine revelation on the twenty-seventh of *Rajab* at the age of forty. The archangel Gabriel descended upon him while he was in the cave *Hara'* in the Meccan mountains, and revealed to him a chapter of the holy Qur'an:

"In the name of Allah, the Beneficent the Merciful. Read in the Name of your Lord Who created ..." The holy Qur'an; The Clot (96): 1.[3]

Prophet Muhammad (S) then started to preach the Divine message to the people of Mecca, saying, *"O people, say that there is no god but Allah, and you will succeed and prosper."*

The Meccans were pagans. They ridiculed at him and caused him great sufferings, to the extent that he said, *"No other prophet suffered as much as I did."* Only a few people from Mecca accepted his Divine message and the first among them was Imam Ali (A) and then the Prophet's wife, Khadija (A) and then a few others.

---

[3] The entire content of the Qur'an was revealed to the Messenger of Allah (S), and this occasion was the first 'official' or 'public' revelation of the Qur'an.

When the pagans' pressures on the new Muslims increased, Prophet Muhammad, (S), left the city of Mecca for the city of Medina. This event marks the starting point of Muslim calendar. In Medina the number of the Muslims increased, and there an Islamic government was formed and it started to grow into a strong government, to the extent that it excelled superseded the world's civilization as well as governments and religions.

During his stay in Medina, the Prophet (S) faced wars and conflicts all of which were because of aggressions by the pagans, Jews and Christians against the Muslims.

In all of those conflicts the Prophet would always adopt the policy of peace, mercy and moral virtues with his enemies. Therefore in all of some eighty such conflicts the total number of casualties on both sides was only one thousand and four hundred, as history has recorded.

From the first day of his Divine mission until his death, various sections of the Qur'an were 'officially' revealed to Prophet Muhammad on various occasions, until this great book was complete (for the people) in twenty-three years.

During this time the holy Prophet formulated and organized the affairs of the Muslims both worldly and all that concern the next life. He taught them the Divine book and wisdom. He formulated rules for their worships, businesses, and for their social, political laws, etc.

Allah, the Most High revealed this verse of the holy Qur'an, *"Today I have perfected your religion for you, completed My grace for you and approved Islam as a religion for you."* - The holy Qur'an (5): 3.

The Messenger of Allah (S) suddenly became seriously ill and died as a result of this particular illness on twenty-eight of *Safar,* year 11 Hijri. Imam Ali (A) undertook the task of preparing the holy Prophet's body for burial. The holy Prophet's body was buried in Medina where his holy shrine stands today.

Rasulollah (meaning Messenger of Allah) (S), always, was a model and an example of the highest standard in sincerity, truthfulness, honesty, high moral abilities, high level of knowledge, forbearance, kindness and forgiving, generosity and bravery, self-control and piety, modesty and virtue, infallibility, justice, humbleness and hard-work.

His physical form was in the best shape and form and his face was bright and attractive. In short, he was the centre of all excellence, the common point of honour and dignity, in him knowledge, justice, and virtue were incorporated. He was the central figure of religion and civilization. There has been no man like him before nor shall there ever be any one like him in the future. This is the Prophet of the Muslims and with him Islam came into existence. His religion is the best of all religions and his book is the best of all books, pure and perfect as Divine guidance for mankind.

Quotes from *Rasulollah* (S)

'The example of my Ahl-ul-Bayt is that of Noah's ark. Whoever boards it is rescued and whoever does not is drowned.'

'O people! I have left behind for you that which if you adhere to, you will never go astray: the Book of Allah (i.e. the Qur'an) and members of my Ahl-ul-Bayt . . .'

'Indeed, He who dies with the love of Aal-Muhammad (the descendants of Muhammad) in his heart, he dies a martyr,

Indeed He who dies with the love of Aal-Muhammad in his heart, he dies and his sins are forgiven,

Indeed, He who dies with the love of Aal-Muhammad in his heart, he dies as a repentant,

Indeed, He who dies with the love of Aal-Muhammad in his heart, he dies as a faithful whose faith has been perfected,

Indeed, He who dies, with the love of Aal-Muhammad in his heart, the angel of death, as well as Munkar and Nakir give him the good news of (him going to) Paradise,

Indeed, He who dies, with the love of Aal-Muhammad in his heart, he is received in Paradise just as a bride is received in her (new) house.'

'Cursed is he who burdens others with his responsibilities and lives off them.'

'On the Day of Judgement, one will not move one step unless he is questioned about four things:

1. *About his life and what he spent it for,*
2. *About his youth and what he used it for,*
3. *About what he earned, where he earned it from, and how he spent it,*
4. *About the love of us, the Ahl-ul-Bayt.'*

'My Lord has recommended nine things to me:

1. *Sincerity in private and in public,*
2. *Justice and equity in contentment and in anger,*
3. *Moderation in poverty and in wealth,*
4. *To forgive he who transgressed against and oppressed me,*
5. *To give to he who deprived me,*
6. *To keep bond with he who severed ties with me,*
7. *To contemplate when I am silent,*
8. *To say Dhikr, remember Allah and His laws, orders and creations when I talk,*
9. *To take heed and learn when I observe.'*

'O Aba Dharr! Value five things before five others:

1. *Value your youth before your old age,*
2. *Value your health before your sickness,*
3. *Value your wealth before your poverty,*
4. *Value your clam (time) before your hectic (time),*
5. *Value your life before your death.'*

4. Leadership of Mankind

(After *Rasulollah*, Prophet Muhammad, (S))

Just as Allah, the Most High, appointed His messengers for the guidance of mankind, in the same way appointing deputies and successors for the prophets was a matter of necessity. Allah, the Most High, appointed twelve distinguished personalities, one after the other, as successors of the holy Prophet of Islam (S).

Rasulollah (S) said:

'I leave with you the two momentous things, as long as you adhere to them you will never go astray - the book of Allah, and my kin the people of my household. Indeed these two will never separate from one another until they arrive at the well (of Kawthar in Paradise).'[4]

Also *Rasulollah* (S) is quoted in Sahih Muslim as saying:

'Islam is established until the day of resurrection, and throughout there will be upon the Muslims twelve caliphs all of whom are from Quraysh.'

Al-Hafiz al-Qanduzi al-Hanafi quotes *Rasulollah* (S) as saying:

'I am the master of the prophets and Ali is the master of the successors, and indeed my successors after me are twelve, the first of whom is Ali and the last is al-Qa'em al-Mahdi.'

These leaders are the twelve Imams (A) who are well known to all Muslims:

1. Imam *Amir-ul-Mu'mineen*, Ali ibn Abi Talib, the holy Prophet's cousin and son in-law, (A).

2. Imam Hassan, son of Imam Ali and Fatimah al-Zahra, daughter of the Prophet, (A).

3. Imam Hussain, the younger son of Imam Ali and Fatimah, daughter of the Prophet, (A).

---

[4] This hadith and many others similar to it have been reported by many Sahabah, and narrators and have been quoted in major references, e.g. the Sihah, such as:
Sahih Muslim, volume 4 page 123, Dar-al-Ma'arif, Beirut.
Musnad Ahmad ibn Hanbal, vol. 3, pp 17, 26, 59, Dar-Sadir, Beirut.
Al-Tirmithi, vol. 5, pp 662-663, Dar-Ihya-al-Turath-al-Arabi, Beirut.

4. Imam *Zayn-ul-Abidin*, Ali son of al-Hussain, (A).

5. Imam *al-Baaqir*, Muhammad son of Ali, (A).

6. Imam *al-Saadiq*, Ja'far son of Muhammad, (A).

7. Imam *al-Kaadhem*, Mussa son of Ja'far, (A).

8. Imam *al-Redha*, Ali son of Mussa, (A).

9. Imam *al-Jawaad*, Muhammad son of Ali, (A).

10. Imam *al-Haadi*, Ali son of Muhammad, (A).

11. Imam *al-Askari*, Hassan son of Ali, (A).

12. Imam *al-Mahdi*, Muhammad son of al-Hassan, The Guided one, The Awaited one, (A).

[Note: All the Imams after Imam Hussain (A) are his descendants. On various occasions *Rasulollah (S)* defined himself, his daughter Fatimah al-Zahra (A), and all these twelve Imams as the *Ahl-ul-Bayt (A)*. Thus every time *Ahl-ul-Bayt* is mentioned only these fourteen infallible individuals are meant.]

The Imams from *Ahl-ul-Bayt* (A) are all the authorities of Allah upon mankind. They all were from the same sacred light out of which the holy Prophet (S) was created. Like the holy Prophet (S) they all were special personalities in matters of knowledge, forbearance, moral excellence, justice, high moral standards and other intellectual achievements as being the successors of the holy Prophet (S) and leaders and Divine guides for mankind.

Describing the role and the significance of *Imam* and *Imamah*, Imam Redha (A) states:

'It is only by the means of the Imamah that Islam is established and its aims achieved. Through it (Imamah) the order of the Muslims is accomplished, the prosperity of the world is attained, and the honour and the glory of the faithful are safeguarded. Imamah is the growing and ongoing root of Islam as well as its exalted branch. It is only through the leadership of the Imam[5] that completeness is attained in daily prayers, Zakat, Fasting, Hajj, Jihaad, tribute, income, executing

---

[5] i.e. the Imam who has been chosen by Allah.

the Hudud and jurisdictions, and safeguarding the borders of the Muslim lands.'

In addition to numerous prophetic hadiths in this respect, there are many verses in the holy Qur'an regarding the vital issue of *Imamah*. One such verse that the above hadith is referring to, and therefore it is supported by, is:

"O Messenger! Proclaim (the Message) that has been revealed to you from your Lord. For if you do not, you would not have fulfilled and proclaimed His Mission!" - The Qur'an: The Table Spread (5): 67.

In this holy verse Allah Almighty is equating the proclamation of a particular Message to the fulfilment of His entire Mission, and Allah warns that failure to make this proclamation is tantamount to failing His entire Mission. This holy verse was revealed to Prophet Muhammad (S) at *Ghadeer Khum* on the 18th of *Dhul-Hajjah* year 10 H, only two months before the death of the Prophet of Islam (S). The particular Message or revelation concerned the appointment of Imam Ali (A) as the immediate successor or caliph of the Messenger of Allah (S). Prophet Muhammad (S) had always, and throughout the 23 years of his mission stated that Ali is his successor. After this revelation, and on direct instructions from Allah Almighty, *Rasulollah* (S) appointed Ali ibn Abi Talib (A) as *Amir-ul-Mu'mineen* and his first caliph and Imam of his *Ummah*[6]. The significance and importance of this appointment is indicated by the comparison Allah Almighty makes between this appointment and the mission of *Rasulollah* (S), which is Islam. In this holy verse Allah Almighty equates the appointment of Imam Ali (A) to the entire mission of *Rasulollah* (S), which is the final revelation for mankind. Furthermore Allah Almighty then goes on to emphasise that without the *Imamah* (of Imam Ali (A)), the *Risalah* of *Rasulollah* (S) is to no avail, and thus the above hadith by Imam Redha (A).

In the following section, a brief biography of them is presented starting with that of the gracious daughter of the holy Prophet (S), Fatimah al-Zahra (A).

---

[6] The title *Amir-ul-Mu'mineen* was exclusively awarded to Imam Ali (A) by *Rasulollah* (S), which means the Commander of the faithful.

Daughter of the Holy Prophet

Fatimah al-Zahra (A) was the daughter of the holy Prophet (S), Muhammad ibn Abdullah and Khadija (A), the great lady and the spiritual mother of the faithful. Fatimah al-Zahra (A) was married to *Amir-ul-Mu'mineen*, Imam Ali ibn Abi Talib (A) and all the Imams are her sons and grandsons and great grandsons.

She was born on 20th of *Jamadi-II* forty-five years after the birth of the holy Prophet (S). She died on Tuesday the 3rd of *Jamadi-II* in the year eleventh of Hijrah (Islamic calendar — when *Rasulollah* migrated from Mecca to Medina). She lived for only eighteen years. Imam Ali (A) prepared her body for burial and did not tell people where her grave was as it was her wish not to tell people where she was buried.

She, like her holy father, possessed all the intellectual abilities and achievements. Many verses of the holy Qur'an were revealed in her praise and about her spiritual credits.

The holy Prophet had given her several honourable titles one of which is, *Sayyedatu Nisaa al-Aalameen* meaning "Leader of the ladies of the worlds".

He loved her immensely. Whenever she would go to her father's house, the holy Prophet (S) would stand up, in her respect, and would give her a special place and kiss her hands and would say, *"Whatever pleases Fatimah, pleases Allah, and whatever angers Fatimah, angers Allah."*

She and Imam Ali had two sons, Imam Hassan and Imam Hussain, and also a third son, Muhsin, who died because of miscarriage resulting from injuries Fatimah al-Zahra (A) sustained[7]. They also had two daughters, Zaynab and Umm Kulthum (A).

Anyone who follows the *sirah* or the way of life of Lady Fatimah al-Zahra (A), would find that this lady is a perfect paradigm, and school in the various domains of life . . . and therefore an ideal exemplar for every woman . . . and man too.

---

[7] When the house of Fatimah al-Zahra (A) was attacked, she sustained horrific injuries, which led to the immediate death of her unborn baby son Muhsin, and her death later. The attack took place only one day after the burial of the body of *Rasulollah* (S). The attack on the house of Fatimah al-Zahra (A) was in aid of dragging Imam Ali (A) out of the house to force him to pay homage to the new ruler.

She was the one who supported her father in his call to Islam, and she, together with a few other faithful believers in the Abi Talib valley, sustained severe hardship perpetrated by the idolaters of Quraysh . . . she was the one who supported *Amir-ul-Mu'minin* Ali (A), who strengthen the foundation of Islam, after the death of the Prophet (S).

She suffered the severe pains and cruelty of the difficult circumstances that surrounded her when she chose the path that leads to the hereafter instead of that leading to this world. She married her cousin *Amir-ul-Mu'minin,* Ali (A) and joined him along with her father *Rasulollah* (S), in the support and strengthening of both the *Risalah* and the *Imamah*, as well as forming the foundation of an Islamic society and conveying the Message of Allah . . . and this is the best model and example Muslim women could possibly follow.

Lady Fatimah (A) divided the duties of their married life with Imam Ali (A). Her responsibility was the duties within the house and his was those without.

Imam Baaqir (A), is reported as saying that:

"Fatimah (A) guaranteed Ali (A) the duties inside the house, (preparing) the dough, (baking) the bread and house keeping. Ali (A) guaranteed Fatimah all that is needed from outside the house, such as providing the firewood and food.

One day he said to her: O Fatimah do you have something (to eat in the house)? She replied: By He who glorified you we do not have anything to give you since three days.

He said: Why did you not inform me?

She said: Rasulollah (S) always advised me against asking you for anything. He said to me 'Do not ask your cousin for anything. If he brought you something, fine! and if not then do not ask him for anything.'

Then Imam Ali (A) left the house (seeking to provide something for the home). He met someone and borrowed one Dinar from him. On his way back, and it was night time, he met Miqdad al-Aswad. He said to Miqdad; What brings you out at this hour? Miqdad replied: By He who has glorified you, it is hunger O Amir-ul-Mu'minin!

The narrator interrupted Imam Baaqir (A) and asked 'and *Rasulollah* was alive (at that time)?' Imam Baaqir (A) replied 'Yes *Rasulollah* was alive.'

Imam Ali (A) said to Miqdad: 'It is what brought me out too. I have borrowed one Dinar which I shall give to you.' And he gave it to him. Imam Ali (A) returned home and found Rasulollah (S) sitting and Fatimah (A) praying and something covered with a cloth between them. When she finished her prayers, she brought that thing which was some bread and meat. He (A) said: O Fatimah! From where this comes to you? She (A) replied: From Allah! Verily Allah provides sustenance to whom He pleases, without measure.

Rasulollah (S) said to Imam Ali (A): Shall I tell you of the like of you and her? Imam Ali (A) replied: Yes.

Rasulollah (S) said: Your example like Zechariah when he came to see Mary in the chamber he found her supplied with sustenance, he asked: **'O Mary! From where this comes to you? She (A) replied: From Allah! Verily Allah provides sustenance to whom He pleases, without measure.** " - The holy Qur'an: The Family of 'Emran (3): 37.

Some of the other attributes that Lady Fatimah decorated herself with, which should be the model for every society and nation who wants to progress forward, are *Zuhd* or non-attachment to material things, kindness and graciousness, altruism and selflessness, perseverance in the face of severe hardship, and many other highly noble characters.

The story of feeding the needy referred to in the holy Qur'an in the *Surah* of Mankind (76) is the best evidence for it. They gave their food, which were only a few pieces of bread to three needy people on three consecutive days. This is after they had vowed to fast three days for Allah for the recovery of their two sons Hassan and Hussain from illness. On the first day, when they wanted to break their fast, a destitute person knocked on the door asking for some food. They all gave all their food, leaving themselves nothing to eat that night. They did the same thing on the next day when an orphan came to their door asking for food, and on the third day in row they gave all their food to a captive who came to them for help. Allah almighty revealed an entire *Surah*, Mankind (76) in this regard praising their conduct. Verse eight of the Surah reads:

'And they feed, for the love of Allah, the indigent, the orphan, and the captive.'

1. Imam Ali

Imam Ali (A) is the son of Abi Talib (A) and Fatimah bint Assad (A). He is the cousin and the son-in-law of the Prophet (S). He was the first successor of the Prophet as leader of mankind and father of all the Imams (A) after him. On instructions from Allah Almighty, *Rasulollah* (S), exclusively awarded Imam Ali (A) the title of *Amir-ul-Mu'mineen*, which means the Commander of the Faithful.

Imam Ali (A) was born inside the holy Ka'abah on Friday the thirteenth of *Rajab*, thirty years after the birth of the holy Prophet (S) and he was fatally wounded by the sword of Abdorrahman ibn Muljim (may the curse of Allah be upon him) on Friday, the nineteenth of *Ramadan* in the Mosque of Kufa and left this world three days latter at the age of sixty three.

His body was prepared for burial by his sons Imam Hassan (A) and Imam Hussain (A) and he was buried in Najaf where his shrine stands today.

His excellent attributes are uncountable. He was the first person to believe in the Messenger of Allah. He never worshipped any idols. In all wars victory depended on his participation and contribution. He never turned his back to the enemy. As a judge, he received this compliment from the holy Prophet, *"Ali is the best judge among you."*

About his vast knowledge the Prophet (S) has said,

"I am the city of knowledge and Ali is the gate of this city"

In relation to his adherence to the Truth the Prophet (S) has said,

"Ali is with the Truth and Truth is with Ali."

He was just in his dealings with people. He treated people equally. He never indulged himself in the worldly matters. He would go to the public treasury and would look at the gold and silver and say, "white (meaning silver) and yellow (meaning gold), attract people other than me." He would then distribute them among the needy. He would treat the destitute with mercy and would accompany the poor and spend time with them and would help people in need. He would speak the truth out loud and issue decrees on the basis of justice.

In short, he was like the holy Prophet (S) in virtuous attributes to the extent that Allah, the Most High, has considered Imam Ali (A) in the holy Qur'an as 'the same' as the Prophet himself (S).

"If anyone disputes with you after the knowledge has come to you (O Muhammad) say: 'Come! Let us summon our sons and your sons, our women and your women, ourselves and yourselves, and then let us earnestly pray and invoke the curse of Allah on those who lie.'"[8] - The Qur'an: The Family of Emran (3): 61.

Rasulollah (S) said: *'He who wants to see Adam's creation, Noah's wisdom, and Ibrahim's perseverance let him look at Ali ibn Abi Talib (A).'*

Taha Hussain, the famous Egyptian writer, states *'I have not heard anything greater than this speech'*, refereeing to *Nahj-ul-Balaghah*, a collection of Imam Ali's speeches, letters, and Words of Wisdom.

Ibn Abi al-Hadeed, the famous historian, states:

'Look at the eloquence and how the words are placed! He manipulates them in such a way to give them both the utter beauty of eloquence and immense influence in the reader.'

Sheikh al-Kulayni states in his book al-Kafi: *'if the entire of the masses of the Mankind and the Jinnkind gathered together to describe*

---

[8] This verse refers to the dispute between the Nazarenes of Najran and Rasulollah (S), and after *Rasulollah* (S) presented all evidence to them and they stubbornly refused to accept all proof of reason, Allah instructed His Messenger through this verse to hold *Ibtihaal* or a 'duel' between the two parties. The 'weapons' needed for such a 'duel' are the most pious individuals of each party. According to this instruction from Allah Almighty, *Rasulollah* (S) summoned the most pious individuals of his party he could possibly get for this 'duel'. They were Imam Hassan and Imam Hussain (the sons), Fatimah (the women), and Imam Ali (the selves). We can see from this act of *Rasulollah* (S), who was complying with the orders of Allah Almighty, that Allah refers to Imam Ali in the holy Qur'an as the 'self of *Rasulollah* (S)'. This goes to show the position and status of Imam Ali in the sight of Allah Almighty. Needless to say when *Rasulollah* (S) summoned these four individuals (the *Ahl-ul-Bayt*) for the 'duel', the Nazarenes saw this array of such individuals, their chief priest said, "I see individuals that Almighty God would answer any prayer or call they make! If you go ahead with this *Ibtihaal*, all the Nazarenes would be annihilated from the face of this earth." They decided therefore to surrender to *Rasulollah* (S).

the concept of unity (of God) in the same way Imam Ali (A) describe it, they would surely fail.'

There are, of course, many sayings and statements made by other notable personalities in various sects and nations, both Muslim and non-Muslim, about the significance of *Nahj-ul-Balaghah* and its relation to our lives.

It was related to me by a friend that during his study at the university of Cambridge, England, the discussion of the professor led him to the topic of *Nahj-ul-Balaghah*, and the professor stated that *'the book of Nahj-ul-Balaghah is such a book that if the world acted upon it, peace would be established throughout it.'* The friend said to the professor *'if so the Muslims should be called upon to practice the teachings in Nahj-ul-Balaghah, to begin with.'* He responded with resentment: *'leave them!'*

I asked *'why?'* And he replied *'if they practiced Nahj-ul-Balaghah our leadership of the world would cease to exist. We are the leaders of the world so long as the Muslims do not practice Nahj-ul-Balaghah, and if one day they practiced Nahj-ul-Balaghah, that day will be the beginning of the end of our leadership of the world.'*

This is *the* fact. Since *Nahj-ul-Balaghah* is not an ordinary book, written by an ordinary person. It is a book of fundamental and universal truths, starting from the knowledge of Allah Almighty, and ending with heaven, and what there is in between lights the torches of free and honourable life. *Nahj-ul-Balaghah* encourages and drives the people towards justice, equality, perseverance, wisdom, progress, and refusing oppression, and therefore it is best fit to be the book of life.

2. Imam Hassan

Imam Hassan (A) is the elder son of Imam Ali (A) and Fatimah al-Zahra (A) daughter of the holy Prophet (S). He is the Prophet's second successor and Imam of the people after Imam Ali. He was born in Medina on Tuesday the fifteenth of *Ramadhan* in the third year of Hijrah. He died, as a martyr because of poison mixed in his food, on Thursday the seventh of *Safar* in the year forty-ninth after

Hijrah. His younger brother, Imam Hussain prepared his body for the burial and he was buried in Baqi' cemetery in Medina.

He excelled all others of his time in worshipping Allah, in knowledge and in spiritual perfections. He was more like the Prophet than other people. He was seen as the most kind-hearted person in his family at his time and the most forbearing amongst the people.

Prophet Muhammad (S) is reported as saying, while hugging his grandson Imam Hassan (A) *'O Allah love him for I dearly love him.'*[9]

The Messenger of Allah (S) used to say about Imam Hassan and his brother Imam Hussain (A):

'they are my sweet basil of this world, whoever loves me should love them, and whoever angers them, he angers me and whoever anger me Allah's anger will be upon him and He enter him in Hell, For they are the masters of the youth of Paradise.'

On many occasions Imam Hassan divided all of his wealth and possession in two; giving one half of it to (the cause of) Allah. He did so to the extent that if he had just one pair of sandals, he gave one of the sandals away and kept the other.

On one occasion Imam Hassan (A) was passing by when he saw a group of destitute people sitting on the ground and eating bread. They invited the Imam to join them and he duly did. He said *'Verily Allah does not like the arrogant.'* When they finished, the Imam (A) then invited them to his hospitality and fed them and gave them clothing.

A man approached Imam Hassan (A) hinting at seeking help from him. In order to save the man the embarrassment of going through his request, the Imam asked him to write down his wishes. On receiving the request letter, the Imam gave him double the amount the man had requested. The people sitting in the vicinity of the Imam said 'what a blissful letter this was for him, O' son of *Rasulollah!*' Imam Hassan (A) said *'its bliss is greater for us, for He has made us the people of nobility. Did you not know that nobility is to give to someone and fulfil his needs while protecting his honour and dignity by sparing him the embarrassment of making his request in detail?'*

---

[9] This hadith has been reported in many sihah and hadith reference books such as sahih Bukhari, Tirmithi, and Muslim, and also in the book of *Bedayah & Nahayah* by Ibn Katheer.

On another occasion a Bedouin man approached Imam Hassan (A) wishing to seek assistance from him . . . the Imam told his assistants to give to the man whatever there was in coffer. There were twenty thousand coins, which they gave to the Bedouin man. The man said lord give me a chance to state my request and praise you . . . replied the Imam (A):

> *We are a people whose grace and grant is spattered,*
> *In which hope and wish revel.*
> *We wish to give abundantly before the request (is made),*
> *Anxious about the honour and dignity of the seeker.*

On another occasion a man from the Shaam district came across Imam Hassan (A). In a massive disinformation campaign by Mu'awiyah, the self-imposed ruler of that district the people of the Shaam have been fed with hatred towards Ali and his descendants. As soon as the man realised that Imam Hassan (A) was nearby, he started to verbally assault and curse the Imam. Imam Hassan (A) remained silent and calm knowing that the Shaami man does not know Ali and his household except through the picture Mu'awiyah son of Hind has painted for them. After the man finished his assault and name calling, Imam Hassan smiled to him and in a calm manner, while totally ignoring what he saw and heard, said:

'May peace be with you "O' Sheikh! I guess you are a stranger in this territory, and you might have mistaken me. If you seek contentment we would gratify you, and if you ask us anything we shall give it to you, and if you sought any guidance from us we shall guide you, if you sought any help from us we shall help you, and if you were hungry we shall feed you, if you needed any clothing we shall give you them, and if you were poor we shall give you money, if you have been expelled (from your home town) we shall accommodate you, and if you had any need we shall fulfil your need . . .'

The Imam continued to offer all the help he could offer the Shaami man showing him grace and kindness. The Shaami man was baffled and totally astonished by the response of the Imam, and he was so ashamed of his conduct that broke in tears saying: *"Allah knows best as to whom He entrust His message with."*

Quotes from Imam Hassan (A)

- *'He who claims he does not like wealth is, to me, a liar, and if his truth is established in this respect, then, to me, he is stupid.'*

- *'Have you seen an oppressor who is more like an oppressed one? The Imam was asked: 'How is that O son of Rasulollah?' The Imam (A) replied: 'He is the jealous person who is in perpetual anguish whereas the envied is in comfort.'*

Imam Hassan (A) used to encourage the people to gain more and more knowledge, and used to say:

- *'Teach others and learn from others' knowledge, in this way you would have perfected your knowledge and learnt things you did not know . . . and to ask a question is half of the knowledge.'*

- *'He who does not have intellect, does not have etiquette, and he who does not have determination, does not have goodwill, and he who does not have a belief does not have morality. The peak of intellect is to socialise with, and treat the people nicely and kindly. Through intellect you can achieve the prosperity of both worlds (this and the hereafter) and without it you would loose all.'*

Someone asked Imam Hassan (A) about politics, the Imam replied

'Politics is to attend to the rights and duties of Allah and to protect the rights of the people; dead or alive. As for the rights of Allah, it is to fulfil what He ordered and abstain from what forbade. And as for the rights of the living it is to discharge your duties towards your Muslim brethrens and not to hesitate serving your community, to be sincere towards Wali-Amr (leader chosen by the people on the basis of his religious credentials) as long as he is sincere to the Ummah, and to raise your objection to him if he deviated from the straight path. As for the rights of the dead, it is to commemorate their good deeds and cover up their bad deeds, for they have their Lord to deal with them.'

3. Imam Hussain

Imam Hussain (A) is the son of Imam Ali (A) and Fatimah (A) daughter of the holy Prophet (S).

He was born in Medina on the third of *Sha'ban*, 3 Hijrah in the same year when his elder brother Imam Hassan was born. He was the Prophet's third successor. He was the leader of the people after his brother Imam Hassan (A).

On the day of *Ashura*, while suffering from extreme thirst, he was brutally martyred by the swords of the army of Yazid ibn Mu'awiyah on Saturday the tenth of *Muharram* in the year sixty-first after Hijrah in *Karbala*. His son Ali Zayn-ul-Abidin (A) prepared his decapitated body, after being left in the field for three days, and buried him in the fields of *Karbala*, Iraq where his shrine stands today.

The holy Prophet has said in the praise of Imam Hassan (A) and Imam Hussain (A):

"My two grandsons are the delights of my eyes."

"Hassan and Hussain are the leaders of the youth in Paradise."

"Hassan and Hussain are both Imams whether they publicly assume the position of leadership or not."

He was the most knowledgeable and the best worshipper among the people of his time. He would pray one thousand Rak'ahs every night like his father, and on many nights he would carry sacks of food to the needy, to the extent that the marks of carrying heavy sacks were clearly visible on his back after his death. He was very kind, had a great and forbearing personality, and was hard on those who disobeyed Allah.

When a Bedouin Arab came to Imam Hussain seeking help he recited the following poem for the Imam:

> *Disappointed will not be he who makes a request from you.*
>
> *For you are generous and trustworthy and your father was the killer of the profligate and the corrupt individuals.*
>
> *If it was not for the former (members) of your (family)[10], we would still have been in hell.*

---

[10] i.e. the Prophet Muhammad, Imam Ali, Lady Faatimah al-Zahra, and Imam Hassan.

Then Imam Hussain (A), while avoiding eye contact with the man, gave him four thousand gold coins (Dinars) and apologized to the man saying:

Take this for I apologise to you, and rest assure that you have my sympathy
For if I were in a different situation and I had more (money) to offer you, I would have given you far more.

Through his courageous revolution, the like of which there has been none in the world, he revived the Islamic Law and the religion of his grandfather, and furthermore he even revived the whole world until the Day of Judgment. He is the leader of the martyrs and the best among people after his elder brother.

Throughout his life the Muslims used to revere and adore Imam Hussain (A), and used to see in him what they had seen in his grandfather, the Messenger of Allah (S). Their adoration for Imam Hussain was not just because he was the grandson of the prophet (S), but also because he was the manifestation of the teachings of Islam and the conducts of the Messenger of Allah (S), no one could fail to see examples of the highest moral qualities in his behaviour.

The holy Prophet has said in the praise of Imam Hussain (A):

"Hussain is from me and I am from Hussain."

Chroniclers and historians have individually remarked that Imam Hussain was the manifestation of the best examples of noble manners and conduct, as well as his vast knowledge, which he inherited from the Messenger of Allah (S). His actions spoke before his words. Imam Hussain (A) was humbly gracious and generous to the poor and those in need. He used to support what is right and fight what was wrong. People always noticed such attributes in his conduct and behaviour as perseverance, forbearance, and magnanimity. He was the most pious and God-fearing of all people of his time.

In his book *Master of the People of Paradise* Dr Ahmad Ashur says:

"If you brows through the pages of the *Sihaah* books you could not fail to come across many tens of hadiths about the merit and superiority of Imam Hussain (A) and the love of the Messenger of Allah (S) for him."

In his book *al-Fusul al-Muhimmah* Ibn al-Sabbagh al-Maliki, quotes Anas ibn Malik who said, "I was with al-Hussain (A) when a servant entered and in her hand a bouquet of basil. She saluted al-Hussain and gave him the bouquet. Al-Hussain (A) said to her 'You are free for the sake of Allah.' I said to al-Hussain 'She gives you a bouquet of basil and salute you and you set her free?' He said *'This is how Allah has taught us! Almighty He says: "If you are saluted, salute back in a better way or return the same salute" and the better way is to set her free.''*[11]

In his Chronicles, Ibn Asaakir reports that Imam Hussain (A) used to receive money (*Khums* and *Zakat*) from Basra and other destinations and he used to distribute the money between the poor and the needy there and then.

Imam Hussain (A) is best known for his revolt against the status quo. By that time the socio-political situation had deteriorated to an extreme and intolerable state, fundamental measures needed to be taken. The main aim and objectives of Imam Hussain's revolt, which are in fact the aim and objectives of Islam at any time and in any place, may be summarised as follows:

- To bring about a responsible community in order to implement and convey the message and teachings of Islam.

- To build an Islamic society which takes Islam as its sole source of reference.

- To rescue the Islamic civilisation from deviation.

---

[11] At the time of the prophet (S) and the Imams (A) slavery was common in the society. One of the most important values in Islam is freedom and therefore it always aimed to gradually eliminate slavery from society. Therefore Islam encouraged people to set their slaves free, and many rewards are prescribed for setting a slave free. The Prophet and the Imams lead the way in this process in two ways. One was to set examples for the Muslims by buying salves and setting them free at the first possible opportunity. The second policy of the Imams was to buy as many salves as they could, educate them and then free them into society as free, well mannered, and responsible adults. In this way, this policy gave a good chance to a slave to attain his/her freedom, set an example for other Muslims to practice, and give less chance to those who wanted to see slavery ripe in society.

This is because the Islamic Ummah or community suffered from various diseases in different domains:

- In the social domain it suffered widely from corruption, bribery, cheating, oppression, favouritism and nepotism.

- From the law and order point of view, the criminal was not being prosecuted, and therefore crime was ripe.

- From the ethical viewpoint, they had turned the moral values upside down.

- From the economic viewpoint, the ruling elite and their cronies monopolised the wealth of the nation.

For such reasons, and for the fact that the Muslims had remained indifferent to these issues to the extent that these had become the norm, that Imam Hussain rose against the injustice and corruption that was being conducted in the name of Islam.

In the course of his jihad in the cause of Allah, Imam Hussain was brutally beheaded and his body mutilated, alongside his sons, relatives, and some seventy of his followers. Furthermore the women and children, who were subsequently captured, including Imam Hussain's sisters Zaynab (A) and Umm Kolthum (A) as well as Zayn-ul-Abidin (A), were taken as prisoners and paraded in towns and villages as villains.

And since then the movement of Imam Hussain (A) inspired the reform movements against despot rulers all over the world and the Muslims continue to reap the fruit of the event of *Karbala* and every year during the month of *Muharram* the memory of *Ashura* is commemorated with vigour by the Muslims all over the world.

4. Imam Zayn-ul-Abidin

Imam Ali Zayn-ul-Abidin (A) is the son of Imam Hussain (A) and Shahe Zanan daughter of Yazdgerd, king of Persia. He was born in Medina on fifteenth of *Jamadi-I* in the year thirty-six after Hijrah, which was the day when Imam Ali liberated the city of Basra, Iraq. He died, because of poison mixed in his food by the enemies of *Ahl-ul-Bayt*, on Saturday, the twenty fifth of *Muharram*, in the year ninety five after Hijrah, at the age of fifty seven and he was buried in *Baqi'* cemetery in Medina.

He excelled all others of his time in knowledge, worshipping Allah, spiritual perfections, piety, and helping the needy. In the matters of the Islamic Shari'a, numerous jurists quote him widely and there are many aspects of words-of-wisdom, spiritual guidance, prayers, and invocations that he left behind as his legacy. Because of his continuous prayers and invocations he became known as *Zayn-ul-Abidin,* meaning the best of the worshipers. He is also known as *al-Sajjaad,* meaning the *prostrater,* for his frequent and prolonged prostration.

Very often at night he would carry money and sacks of food to the needy with his face covered by a mask so that no one would recognise him. When he left this world, then people of Medina realised that the person who used to deliver to them food etc. with his face covered by a mask, was none other than Imam *Zayn-ul-Abidin.* He loved to see the orphans and destitute join him for his dinner or lunch.

Every month he would call upon his servants and would offer them help if any of them needed to get married or if anyone wanted to be set free. Whenever a needy person would come to him asking for help he would say this, *"welcome to those who carry for me supplies to the next life."*

It is said that he would pray a thousand Rak'ahs of prayer in every twenty-four hours. At the time of prayer his face would change, and he would shiver like a leaf out of his realisation the greatness of Allah, the Most High. Due to his prostrating so much before Allah his forehead and knees were clearly marked.

Once a person from his relatives spoke rudely to him using offending words such that normally would hurt one's feelings. The Imam patiently waited for the person to finish then the Imam stood up and stepped nearer to the person, and recited this verse from the holy Qur'an, *"... and those who control their anger and forgive people, Allah loves those who do good."* The Family of Emran (3): 134.

He then said to that person, *"Brother, I heard all that you said to me. If all that you said about me is true, then I ask Allah to forgive me and if all that you said about me is not true, then may Allah forgive you."*

In the course of his supplications which he became best known for, Zayn-ul-Abidin (A) left behind a magnificent intellectual and doctrinal masterpiece known as the *Sahifah al-Sajjaddeyyah*. Of course the *Sahifah* does not include all of his supplications, as many others are found in other reference books.

The supplications of Imam Zayn-ul-Abidin (A) are well known for their immense influence on the soul of the reader, and that of the listener. The choice of words and meaning of the supplications move the reader in such a way that change one's life and give his life purpose and direction.

The collection of the supplications of Zayn-ul-Abidin (A) is a great school for he who seeks the truth. It is a school, which points to the love, wisdom and power of Allah Almighty. It points man to the values and the qualities of the teachings of Islam. It teaches him how to repent and how to talk to Allah.

Imam Zayn-ul-Abidin (A) is also responsible for the creation of the book of rights, which includes fifty fundamental rights one has, or is responsible for. This book of rights served as a guide to the Muslims as well as a challenge to the society and the ruling circumstances.

In his book Manaqib, Ibn Shahr Ashub reports that Imam Zayn-ul-Abidin (A) received some guests, and the servant was rushing to serve the guests when some of the hot cooking cutlery fell on the Imam's child, killing him. The servant was extremely disturbed and frightened. When the Imam saw him in that state said to him *'You did not intend this! Go for you are free for the sake of Allah.'*

Zayn-ul-Abidin (A) used to buy a thousand slaves at a time and then he used to educate them with the teachings of Islam and within a year free them into the society as well mannered, educated, and honourable members of the society. It is reported that he directly bought, educated and freed some fifteen thousands slave during his lifetime.

Quotes from Imam Zayn-ul-Abidin (A)

Imam Zayn-ul-Abidin (A) said to his son, al-Baaqir (A): *'Do good to whoever seeks it from you. For if he deserved it then you have achieved your goal, and if he did not deserve it, you are the kind to do so. If someone swore at you, and he is on your right hand side, and then, turns to your left, and apologised to you, accept his apologies.'*

On the subject of trustworthiness and honesty, Imam Zayn-ul-Abidin (A) says: *'By He who sent Muhammad (S), with the Truth (I swear that) if the killer of my father al-Hussain (A) entrusts me with the sword which he killed him (A) with, I would return it back to him.'*

5. Imam al-Baaqir

Imam Muhammad Al-Baaqir (A) is the son of Ali ibn al-Hussain (A) and Fatimah daughter of Imam Hassan (A). He was born on Monday the third of *Safar* (also reported to be first of *Rajab*) in the year fifty seven, after Hijrah and he died, because of poison given to him by the enemies of the *Ahl-ul-Bayt*, on Monday the seventh of *Dhilhajjah* in the year one hundred twenty four at the age of fifty seven and he was buried in the Baqi' cemetery in Medina.

Imam Muhammad Al-Baaqir (A) was a man of great virtue and leadership, a man of vast knowledge, great forbearance, great moral discipline, worship, generosity, and kindness.

A Christian man, mispronouncing Imam's name, once said to him, "Are you *Baqar*? (meaning, a 'cow'). The Imam said, "No, I am *Baaqir*." The man then said, "Are you the son of a female cook?" The Imam said, "that is her profession." The man then said, "Are you the son of the bad Negro woman?" The Imam said, "if what you say is true, then may Allah forgive her and if what you say is not true then may Allah forgive you." This transformed the Christian man, and he became a Muslim.

Imam Muhammad Al-Baaqir (A) had profound knowledge and he would answer every question when asked without delay. Ibn Ata of Mecca has said this about the Imam, "I never saw the scholars look so small as they did in the presence of Imam Muhammad Baaqir. I saw al-Hakam ibn Utaybah, with all his prestige in the community, looked just like a child in the presence of Imam Muhammad Baaqir."

Muhammad ibn Muslim said, "I asked Imam Muhammad Al-Baaqir all the questions that would come to my mind, until I had asked him about thirty thousand *Hadiths*."

Imam al-Baaqir used to recite the names and attributes of Allah continuously. His son Imam Ja'far al-Saadiq has said, *"My father would recite Allah's names very often and even when walking he would keep reciting Allah's names and people's talking to each other would not distract him from reciting Allah's names. He would pray for long hours at night and his tears would flow tremendously during his worshipping."*

Imam al-Baaqir (A) may be credited to have established the first Islamic university in the history of Islam. Given the turmoil in political situation of the time, the Umayyad rulers had less to suppress Imam al-Baaqir (A) and therefore Imam al-Baaqir (A) had more breathing space to teach those who sought the teachings of Islam in the sciences of the Qur'an, *Fiqh*, doctrine, etc.

Quotes from Imam al-Baaqir (A)

'The practice of Islam is founded on five mattrer: the upholding of the daily prayers, the purification of the wealth (giving the Khums and Zakat), performing the Hajj pilgrimage, the Fasting during the holy month of Ramadahn, allegiance to the authority (wilayah) of the us the Ahl-ul-Bayt. Exceptions are given in four of them but none is given for the wilayah. He who does not possess sufficient wealth, does not give Khums/Zakat. He who does not possess sufficient wealth, is not obliged to go to Hajj. He who is ill can perform the daily prayers in sitting mode, and does not fast during the month of Ramadahn. However the wilayah is obliged upon him regardless of his health and wealth.'

'Three are amongst the noble values of this world and the hereafter: To forgive he who transgresses against you, To bond ties with he who severs ties with you, To forbear he who insults you.'

'The most regretting individual on the Day of Judgement is he who preaches for others to do good but does not practices it himself.'

'He who says the truth, his acts would be purified, and he whose intention is good, his sustenance will be increased, and he who is kind to his family his lifespan would increase.'

'He who teaches guidance, will have a reward similar to the rewards of all of those who act upon it without reducing anything from their reward. He who teaches misguidance, will have a punishment similar to the punishments of all of those who act upon it without reducing anything from their punishment.'

28

6. Imam al-Saadiq

Imam Ja'far al-Saadiq (A) is the son of Imam Muhammad Al-Baaqir (A) and Fatimah also known as Umm Farwah. He was born in Medina on Monday the seventeenth of *Rabi'-I* in the year eighty-three after Hijrah. He died, because of poison given to him by the enemies of *Ahl-ul-Bayt (A)*, on twenty-fifth of *Shawwal* in the year one hundred forty eight after Hijrah at the age of sixty-five.

Imam Ja'far al-Saadiq (A) unquestionably possessed vast knowledge, wisdom, piety, simple living manners, truthfulness, and justice. Sheikh al-Muffid[12] has said that from none of the members of the family of the holy Prophet so much Hadith is narrated as much as it is narrated from the sixth Imam. None of the members of the family of the holy Prophet had the chance to teach so many of the narrators of Hadith or historians as did Imam Ja'far al-Saadiq (A). A list of the names of the narrators of Hadith from Imam Ja'far al-Saadiq (A) number about four thousand among whom is Abu Hanifah, the founder of the Hanafi school, who was Imam Saadiq's student too.

Imam Ja'far al-Saadiq (A) lived a simple life. He himself would work in his garden. He would pray extensively and with great deal of attention and concentration to the extent that he would loose consciousness.

One night Rashid, the ruler of the time wanted to meet him and he sent one of his servants to the house Imam Ja'far al-Saadiq (A). The servant has said that he found the Imam in the state of prostration before Allah with his hands and face on the ground and his forehead and the sides of his face dust on them.

Imam Ja'far al-Saadiq (A) was very generous, of excellent moral perfections and of very polite manners in his social dealings.

Like his father (A) Imam Saadiq (A) lived during a period when the political situation was going through turbulence stages and therefore

---

[12] Abu Abdullah Muhammad al-Harithi al-Baghdadi, known as sheikh al-Muffid, and also ibn al-Mu'allim, 336-413 H, 948-1022. He is one of the foremost figures of Shi'a history. A student of ibn Babuyah al-Qummi, the great teacher of theology in the 4th/10th century, sheikh al-Muffid was in turn the teacher of such celebrated Shi'a theologians as sheikh al-Murtadha. The author of some 170 treatises concerned almost completely with theology, jurisprudence, hadith, and sacred history, sheikh al-Muffid soon became one of the main figures of the Shi'a scholars.

the rulers did not have the time to target the Imam to the extent that prevent him from any activity. This gave Imam al-Saadiq (A), just like his father, the opportunity to continue the task Imam al-Baaqir (A) started, which was the setting up of the Islamic university and the teaching of Islamic sciences such as Qur'an, Fiqh, etc. It is reported that more than four thousand scholars graduated from the school of Imam Ja'far al-Saadiq (A), and between them, up to ninety thousand hadiths have been reported from Imam Saadiq (A).

Quotes from Imam al-Saadiq (A)

'Nothing other than three matters continue to bring an individual rewards after death. A charity that Allah helped him establish during his life, and this (charity) continues after his death, a good practice acted upon (by others), and an offspring who prays for him.'

'The right of a Muslim upon another is that he is not full when his brother goes hungry, and he does not quench his thirst when his brother is thirsty, and he is not clothed when his brother is naked, it is most great the right of a Muslim upon his brother.'

'Love for your Muslim brother what you love for yourself.'

'Amongst the manners of the ignorant is to answer before he hears (the argument), and to oppose before he understands, and to give a judgement upon what he does not know.'

'He who acts not in accordance with a vision, is like he who is going down the wrong way, and speeding does not give him anything other than distancing him further from the truth.'

'The most beloved of my brothers to me is he who presents me my mistakes.'

'Seventy sins of the ignorant are forgiven before one is forgiven for the scholar.'

'Make bonds with he who sever ties with you, give to he who denies you, be kind to he who was bad to you, salute he who swore at you, be fair and just to he who fought you, forgive he who oppressed you; just as you would like to be forgiven, learn from Allah when He forgives you; do you not see the sun shines upon the believers and the non-believers, and the rain comes down upon the good and the bad?'

7. Imam al-Kaadhem

Imam Mussa al-Kaadhem (A) is the son of Imam Ja'far al-Saadiq (A) and Hamida. He was born in Abwa between Mecca and Medina on Sunday the seventh of *Safar*, in the year one hundred twenty eight after Hijrah. He died, because of poison, in Haroon's Jail after fourteen years of unjust and hostile confinement therein, on twenty-fifth of *Rajab*, in the year one hundred eighty three.

His body was prepared for burial by his son Imam Ali al-Redha (A) and was buried where his shrine stands today in Kaadhemiah, Iraq. He was the most knowledgeable person of his time and the best of them. He was very generous, brave and of excellent spiritual perfections and worship extensively and prolonged prostrations in the presence of Allah. His control over his anger was as such that he became known as *al-Kaadhem*, which means one who curbs one's anger.

Imam Mussa al-Kaadhem (A) was renowned for his knowledge in various fields, to the extent that he dazzled the people. In one case the Imam entered in a debate with the famous Christian scholar 'Borayha'. At the end of the debate, the latter was overwhelmed by the arguments and answers the Imam had presented. As a result Borayha embraced Islam and became a devoted Muslim.

Once a poor person asked him for some help and the Imam, in order to know the man's attitude of mind, asked him some questions. When the man answered them properly, the Imam in appreciation of alertness of the man gave him two thousand Dirhams (gold coins) instead of the hundred that he had asked for.

He had the most beautiful voice in reciting the holy Qur'an. His love of worshipping Allah and prolonged prostration before Him was so much that he breathed his last during his prostration before Allah.

The Abbasids forced their way to power after the bloody overthrow of the previous tyrant rulers, the Umayyads, who had ruthlessly fought the *Ahl-ul-Bayt* throughout their rule. The Abbasids had come to power with the pretext of seeking to support the *Ahl-ul-Bayt* relief their suffering under the banner of *'Ya le-Tharat al-Hussain'* meaning 'Seeking the revenge of al-Hussain'. When they established themselves on the throne government and had a good grip of power, the Abbasids turned their attention to the *Ahl-ul-Bayt* and started to fight them even more oppressively than the Umayyads.

After the martyrdom of his father, al-Imam al-Saadiq (A) at the hands of the Abbasids, Imam al-Kaadhem assumed the office of the Imamah, and subsequently he spent most of his latter part of life until his martyrdom in the prison of the Abbasids.

Quotes from Imam al-Kaadhem (A)

'Allah has given the people two proofs, an apparent one and a hidden one. The apparent one is His messengers, prophets and Imams, and the hidden one is the intellect.'

'Learn thoroughly the Teachings of Islam for this learning is the key to the (correct) vision, perfect worship, the means to elevated stations, honourable ranks in this world and the hereafter. For the merit of the Faqeeh (scholar) over the worshiper is that of the sun over the planets. And he who does not seek knowledge about his religion, none of his achievements would be accepted by Allah.'

'Endeavour to divide your time into four categories: one for the supplication with Allah, another to make a living, the third for socialising with the brethrens and those trustworthy individuals who are honest to you and point out to you your mistakes in confidence, and the fourth to seek in seclusion non-forbidden pleasures, and with this you gain strength and vigour for the other three.'

'. . . and the believer is the brother of the believer even if not born by the same parents. Cursed is he who accuses his brother, cursed is he who cheats his brother, cursed is he who does not admonish and advise his brother, cursed is he who backbites his brother.'

'He whose two days are equal is a looser, and he whose second day is worse than his first is cursed. He who does not observe progress in himself is in retreat and he who is in retreat, death is better for him than life.'

Addressing one of his disciples:

'O Hishaam! If you had a nut in your hand and the people said you have a pearl, it would be of no benefit to you and you know it is a nut. And if you had a pearl in your hand and the people said you have a

nut in your hand, it would be of no detriment to you and you know that it is a pearl.'

'Any word of wisdom is sought for by the faithful Muslim, so always seek knowledge . . .'

8. Imam al-Redha

He is Imam Ali al-Redha (A), son of Imam Mussa al-Kaadhem (A) and al-Sayyidah Najmah. He was born on Friday the eleventh of *Thilqa'dah*, in the year one hundred forty eight in Medina and he died, because of poison mixed in his food by the enemies, on the last day of *Safar* in the year two hundred and three. His body was prepared for burial by his son Imam Muhammad al-Jawaad (A) and he was buried in Khurasan, Iran where his shrine stands now.

It is needless to speak of his achievements in knowledge, virtue, nobility, generosity, moral perfections, humbleness, and worship of Allah.

Ma'mun, the ruler of the time asked him to take charge of the administration of the Muslim government but he did not accept it because he knew that things will not go the way he wanted them to go. It was just like the case of his great grandfather Imam Ali, *Amir-ul-Mu'mineen (A)*, who did not accept the post of leadership with the condition that he runs the government according to the policies of the two sheikhs, i.e. Abu Bakr and Omar. Imam Ali (A) said that he would run the government according to the Book of Allah and the Sunnah of Rasulollah (S), but not according to the policies of the two sheikhs, but Othman did.

When Imam Ali al-Redha (A) did not accept the post of the leadership of the government, Ma'mun asked him to be his successor and the Imam accepted it with the condition that he would not be asked to take part in any governmental tasks during the lifetime of Ma'mun.

Examples of the vast knowledge of Imam Ali al-Redha (A) came to light when Ma'mun invited him and scholars from various religions and different schools of thought to attend a seminar of debate over the theological issues and matters of the doctrines of faith. History books report the details of the debates that took place between the Imam and the other scholars and how Imam Ali al-Redha (A) provided convincing and irrefutable proofs and evidence to their questions and arguments.

For his worship he would stay many nights awake in prayers and worship and would complete reading the holy Qur'an in three days. Very often he would pray a thousand Rak'ahs in twenty-four hours, with prolonged prostrations lasting many hours and he would fast very often. He was very generous and he would help people during the night so that no one would recognize him.

He never did any injustice to any one in words or deeds. He would never speak very loud or rough. He never sat leaning on some thing or laugh loudly. He would call upon all the members of his family and servants to have dinner or lunch together.

Quotes from Imam al-Redha (A)

'Pay visit to each other (Socialise with one another), so that you get friendlier.'

'He who repents is as he who has no sin.'

'Cleanliness and hygiene is one of the traits and manners of the prophets.'

'The most superior knowledge is the knowledge of the self.'

'(In the Qur'an) Allah has commanded (us to do) three things which are linked to another three. He ordered (us to perform) the daily prayers and Zakat, and he who performs the prayers but not the Zakat, his prayers would not be accepted. He ordered (us) to be thankful to Him and to the parents, and he who is not thankful to his parents is not thankful to Allah. He ordered (us) to be pious and have fear of him, and keep close ties with the relatives, and he who does not keep close ties with his relatives is not pious.'

'He who likens Allah to His creations is a Mushrik (polytheist), and he who attributes to Him something which He has forbidden is a Kafir (infidel).'

'The merit of Emaan (faith) is a grade higher than that of Islam (Submission to Allah's will), and the merit of Taqua (Fear-of-Allah) is a grade higher than that of Emaan, and the merit of Yaquin (conviction) is a grade higher than that of Taqua, and the sons of Adam (or human beings) are not given anything better than Yaquin.'

'Emaan has four pillars: Trusting and relying on Allah, Contentment and pleasure with the will of Allah, Submittance to the ordinance of Allah, and Delegation and turning over (the affairs) to Allah.'

'Emaan is to discharge the obligatory duties and to refrain from committing forbidden acts. Emaan is recognition by heart, admission by tongue, and practicing, by all limbs, everything that has been ordered.'

'The Qur'an is the sturdy rope of Allah and His firm grip, and His perfect road that leads to paradise, and delivers from the fire. It does not pall despite the passing of aeons, and does not dissipate despite being oft repeated, because it was not created for one time rather than another but as the argument and proof for all humanity. Falsehood does not approach it from before it or behind it, a revelation from The All Wise, The All Praised.'

A narrator reports, I asked Imam al-Redha (A) 'What do you say about the Qur'an?' Imam Redha (A) replied: *'It is the word of Allah, and so do not surpass it, and do not seek guidance in anything else, for you will be deviated and go astray.'*

9. Imam al-Jawaad

Imam Muhammad al-Jawaad (A) is the son of Imam Ali al-Redha (A) and al-Sayyidah Subaika. He was born on the tenth of *Rajab* in the year one hundred and ninety-five after the Hijrah in Medina. He died, because of poison given to him by the enemies of *Ahl-ul-Bayt* (A), in Baghdad at the end of *Thilqa'dah* in the year two hundred and twenty and he was buried next to the grave of his grandfather in Kaadhemiah Iraq where his shrine stands now.

Imam Muhammad al-Jawaad (A) excelled all others of his time in knowledge, spiritual perfection, generosity, social, and moral manners, and dealings and in the art of eloquent communications.

He would carry gold and silver with him to be spent for the needy. If he was asked for assistance by any of his uncles or aunts Imam al-Jawaad (A) would give them between 25 to 50 gold coins.

More people became aware of the vast knowledge of Imam al-Jawaad (A) when some eighty scholars from different places met with him on his way back from Hajj and asked him all sorts of questions, to all of which the Imam provided convincing and irrefutable answers. It is astonishing indeed that once people gathered around him to ask him all sorts of questions, which numbered around thirty thousand, and he answered all of them correctly and at that time he was only nine years old. Age factor, however, was never an issue in the case of the members of the family of the Prophet.

In appreciation to the Imam's station, the ruler of the time gave to him his daughter in marriage after the Imam answered all the questions that the Caliph had asked him for trial purposes.

Quotes from Imam al-Jawaad (A)

'He who trusts upon Allah, He guides him to felicity and happiness.

He who depends upon Allah, He suffices him the matters of his life.

The trust in Allah is a fortress where no one other than the trustworthy believer is housed.

Reliance on Allah is salvation from all evil and protection from all enemies.

Islam is a source of honour.

Knowledge is treasure.

Silence is light.

The utmost degree of Zuhd (abstinence) is avoiding sin.

There is no destruction for Islam like innovations (heresy).

Nothing is more decadent for man then greed.

Through (the pious) ruler the people are guided.

Through supplication calamities are repelled. . . . '

'If the ignorant keeps silent, people would not differ.'

'As the beneficences of Allah upon a person increase, the needs of the people towards him enhance. Thus he who does not meet those needs, exposes those beneficences to annihilation.'

'You should know that you never go out of sight of Allah, so watch in what state you are.'

'The one who commits aggression and tyranny, and the one who helps him to it, and the one who condones it, they are all partners in crime.'

'Forbearance is the garment of the scholar, make sure you clothe yourself with it.'

'The believer needs three qualities; facility from Allah, self-admonishing, and acceptance of constructive criticism.'

'Three practices enable an individual to reach the pleasure and approval of Allah Almighty:

Frequent repentance, leniency, and giving to charity regularly.

And (there are) three qualities which if one possesses, he would never regret: avoiding hastiness, consulting (with others), and to rely on Allah once a decision is made.'

10. Imam al-Haadi

Imam Ali al-Haadi (A) is the son of Imam Muhammad al-Jawaad (A) and al- Sayyidah Samanah. He was born in Medina on fifteenth of *Thilhajjah* (also reported as second of *Rajab*) in the year two hundred and two after Hijrah. He died, because of poison given to him by the enemies, in Samarra, Iraq on Monday the third of *Rajab* in the year two hundred fifty four after the Hijrah and he was buried in Samarra where his shrine stands today.

Imam al-Haadi (A) remarkably excelled all others of his time in the fields of human perfections, as knowledge, generosity, politeness of manners, worshipping Allah, moral qualities, and discipline.

One example of his generosity is the case of the ruler of his time sending him thirty thousand Dirhams that he (A) gave the lot to an Arab from Kufa, saying, *"pay your debts out of it and spend the rest on your family and relatives and accept our apologies."* The man, thanking the Imam, said, "sir, the debts on me are only about one third of it but Allah knows who to entrust with His message of Divine guidance."

Quotes from Imam al-Haadi (A)

'Better than the good-deed is he who performs it.

37

More striking than the beautiful words is he who says them.
More worthy than knowledge is he who conveys it.
More evil than evil is he who causes it.
More frightening than fear is he who brings it.'

*'Allah cannot be defined except with what he has defined himself.
How can He be defined when wits are unable to perceive Him,
imaginations fail to reach Him, minds cannot explain Him, and the
visions cannot encompass Him?'*

*'When justice is dominant, one may not suspect another unless he is
sure of his suspicion about him, and when injustice is dominant, one
should not assume good thing about another unless he is sure of it.'*

'Jealousy erodes the good deeds and brings about the bad fortunes.'

*'Beware of jealousy for it will work against you and will have no
effect on your foe.'*

'Indeed, both the scholar and the student share in prosperity.'

*'Allah has made the world a place of calamity and the hereafter a
place of outcome. He has set the calamities of the world to be the
cause of the reward of the hereafter, and has made the reward of the
hereafter a substitute for the calamities of the world.'*

*'Self-conceit restrains (one) from seeking knowledge and brings
about scorn and ignorance.'*

11. Imam al-Askari

Imam Hassan al-Askari (A) is the son of Imam Ali al-Hadi (A) and al-
Sayyidah Jiddah. He was born on Monday the tenth of *Rabi'-II* in the
year two hundred thirty two after the Hijrah. He died, because of
poison given to him by the enemies of *Ahl-ul-Bayt* (A), on Friday the
eighth of *Rabi-I*. His body was prepared for burial by his son Imam
al-Mahdi and he was buried next to the grave of his father in Samarra
where his shrine stands now.

His noble qualities such as his knowledge, generosity, perfect
manners, servitude to Allah and excellent personality are well known.
His physical form was perfectly shaped and spiritually he was just
like his great grand father the holy Prophet.

Someone called Ismael narrates:

"Once I sat on the way waiting for the Imam to pass by and when he did I complained about my difficulties and asked him for financial help. The Imam said, "You swear by Allah falsely while you have buried 100 Dinars as a saving! What I say is not to deny you financial help." Then the Imam called upon his servant to give him all he had. The servant gave me 100 Dinars."

Having heard about his grace and generosity, a man, who needed 500 Dirhams, approached Imam al-Askari (A) and the Imam gave him 500 Dirhams, and another 300 Dirhams on top of that.

He was perceived by the Christians of the time as having all the human perfections and qualities such as knowledge, virtues, and miracles like Jesus was believed to have had.

The Imam was known for his prolonged worship to Allah as well as his nobility and majesty.

Quotes from Imam al-Askari (A)

'No respectful individual abandons the truth unless he becomes debased, and no abject individual pursues the truth unless he becomes honourable.'

'He who advices and criticises his brother covertly, has decorated him. He who does so in public has rebuked him.'

'The best of your brothers is the one who forgets your sins and remembers your favour to him.'

'The heart of the fool is in his mouth, and the mouth of the wise is in his heart.'

'He who uses false means to achieve his ends would regret his policy.'

'Rage is the key to every evil.'

'It is sufficient politeness and courtesy for you to refrain from what you dislike to see from others.'

'Be cautious about seeking fame and power (for the sake of notoriety) for they lead to annihilation.'

12. Imam al-Mahdi

Imam Muhammad al-Mahdi, al-Hujjah - the authority - is the son of Imam Hassan al-Askari and al-Sayyidah Nargis. He was born in Samarra, Iraq, on fifteenth of *Sha'ban*, in the year two hundred fifty five after Hijrah.

His birth was kept secret, since the authorities of the time were actively seeking to terminate his birth, or eliminate him immediately if he is found alive. [The circumstances of his birth are similar to those of Prophet Moses (A), when the then authorities were actively seeking the baby who would grow to bring about the end of the rule of Pharaoh.]

He is the last of the Imams of the people on earth and with him the line of succession to the holy Prophet ends. He still, by the will of Allah is living in this world but he does not appear in public. He will declare himself to the public, by the orders of Allah, at a time when the earth will be filled with injustice and he will restore order and make justice prevail.

The holy Prophet and the other Imams have said that Imam al-Mahdi will live so long until he will have full control of the whole world, make justice to prevail and will do away with all tyranny – "He will make Allah's religion to triumph even though the polytheist should resent it."

Aba Sa'id al-Khidri reports that when Rasulollah (S) was ill, which led to his death, Fatimah al-Zahra (A) entered the room he was laying in to nurse him (S) and I was sitting on the right of Rasulollah (S). Noticing his weakness Fatimah (A) was upset by his state she started to cry. Rasulollah (S) said to her (A):

'Why do you cry O Fatimah? Do you not know that Allah sought for the best on earth and chose your father as His Messenger, and then sought again He chose your husband and advised me to marry him to you and instructed me to appoint him as my successor. Do you not know that by the grace of Allah upon you, Allah married you to the most knowledgeable of all, and the most forbearing of all, and the foremost of all having the faith of Islam? Fatimah (A) smiled and Rasulollah (S) went on to inform her about what Allah has given to the Ahl-ul-Bayt (A) by saying:

Allah has given us we the Ahl-ul-Bayt six qualities which have not been given to anyone before us and or to anyone after us the Ahl-ul-Bayt.

1. *Our prophet is the best of the prophets and he is your father,*

2. *and our Wasi, or caliph, is the best Wasi and he is your husband,*

3. *and our martyr is the best martyr and he is your father's uncle Hamzah,*

4. *and from us is al-Hassan the Sibt (grandson of the prophet) of this Ummah, and he is your son,*

5. *and from us is al-Hussain the Sibt (grandson of the prophet) of this Ummah, and he is your son,*

6. *and from us is the Mahdi, Saviour, of this Ummah, behind whom Jesus will pray.*

Then the prophet patted the shoulder of al-Hussain (A) and said 'and from him is the Mahdi of this Ummah''

Ibn Abbas reports that Rasulollah (S) said:

'Indeed Ali ibn Abi Talib is the Imam of my Ummah and my caliph and successor upon this Ummah after me, from his sons is the Qa'im (al-Mahdi) the Awaited, who would fill the world with justice after it had been overcome by tyranny and injustice. By He who sent me with Truth as a Bearer of glad tidings and a Warner, those who remain steadfast and believe in him are dearer than red sulphur.

Then Jaber ibn Abdullah al-Ansari stood up and asked: 'O Rasulollah! Will the Qa'im from your descendants go into an occultation?' Rasulollah (S) replied,

'Yes by my Lord. For Allah shall test and purify the believers and wipe out the non-believers. O Jaber! This matter is one of the secrets of Allah, hidden from the servants of Allah. Thus I warn you about doubting about this for doubting the wish of Allah is Kufr (unbelief).'

As this great Imam went into occultation, by the order of Allah, during the period he was living in his house in Samarra, the Muslims, out of devotion to this Imam, consider his house as a sacred place.

May Allah, give him permission to appear in public very soon and let us be of his supporters and helpers.

Quotes from Imam al-Mahdi (A):

'Allah Almighty sent Muhammad peace be upon him as a Mercy to the worlds, and with him He perfected His beneficence, and sealed His prophets, and He sent him (with His message) to all people (to come).'

'My benefit (to the people) during my occultation is similar to that of the sun when it disappears from sight behind the clouds.'

'I am the Mahdi, and I am the leader of the time, I am the one who would fill it (the earth) with justice after it has been overcome with injustice and aggression. Indeed the earth never remains without a Proof and Authority (of Allah).'

'. . . and if Allah give us the permission of speech, then truth will manifest and falsehood would disappear.'

'Allah insists that eventually Truth must hold and Falsehood must decline.'

'Nothing like the daily prayers forces the nose of the Satan to the ground, so perform the daily prayers and force his nose to the ground.'

5. *Resurrection*

Resurrection means that Allah, the Most High, will one day bring back to life all the dead people to let every one find the results of their deeds whether good or bad. Those who were praying, fasting, speaking the truth, maintaining sincerity, giving shelters to the orphans and feeding the destitute etc., they will be admitted into Paradise wherein streams would flow and will enjoy the mercy of Allah and the pleasures of Paradise. But those who disbelieved, committed evil deeds, spoke lies, breached their trust, committed murders, stole others' properties, committed adultery or consumed intoxicant substances etc., will go to Hell to suffer all the miseries therein forever.

Before Paradise and Hell there are two other stations:

1. The Grave, wherein every one will be questioned about his or her deeds and the person will be treated in accordance with the quality of his deeds. Because of this the holy Prophet said, "the grave will either be a pit of the pits of Hell or a garden of the gardens of Paradise." People's condition in the grave would be similar to one's condition when dreaming during one's sleep, in which one would either have pleasant dreams or bad and terrifying ones. Another person awake does not realize whether the sleeping person is having bad dreams or good ones, in the same way we do not realize whether a dead person is happy or not.

2. Resurrection will take place after these bodies are brought back to life from their graves. All people will be brought together at one place wherein the court of Justice and the Balance will be established. The Judges are the prophets and the good servants of Allah and everyone's records of deeds will be made public. The witnesses will be present, good people will be saved and people with evil deeds will face the consequences.

One, must, therefore take all the necessary steps to protect him/herself against bad consequences of evil deeds and the terrifying sufferings of the life to come, which will never end.

THE HOLY QUR'AN

The Need to Learn and Teach the Holy Qur'an

Praise to Allah and may peace and blessings of Allah be with the holy Prophet and his family.

In the following we quote some Hadiths (sayings of the holy Prophet) from the book *Wasa'el al-Shi'a*, on the topic of the holy Qur'an.

Sa'ad al-Khaffaf has narrated from Imam Saadiq (A) as saying, *"Sa'ad, learn the holy Qur'an, because on the day of judgment the holy Qur'an will come in the best form that people may have ever seen.*

(The Imam continued) *...until the holy Qur'an comes to Allah, the Most high, and Allah addressing the Qur'an says, "My true spoken words and authority on earth, look up and ask for your wishes. Your wishes shall be granted and your intercession shall be accepted. How did you find my servants?" The holy Qur'an replies, "My Lord, some of them kept my teachings and did not lose anything from me, but some of them lost me and disrespected me and did not believe me even though I was your authority to your creatures." Allah then replies, "I swear by My Majesty, Greatness and Highness that today I shall give the best reward for your sake, and I shall punish severely because of you."*

The Imam (A) continued, *"One of our followers then will come forward and the Qur'an will say to him, "do you know me? I am the Qur'an for which you kept awake the whole night and faced sufferings in your life. Come let us go to Almighty Allah." The Qur'an then will say, "Lord, this your servant was very close to me and very careful about me. He would love others because of me and would hate others just because of me." Allah, the most High, will then say, "Let my servant enter Paradise and let him be dressed from the garments of the heaven and be crowned." Then he is presented to the Qur'an. Then the Qur'an is asked "Are you happy with the rewards given to your friend?" The Qur'an will say, "Lord, I see this as small reward, give him all the good things." Allah then will say, "I swear by my Majesty, Honour and Highness I shall reward him and others like him with five things with all the good things: I shall give them eternal youth, health, richness, happiness and life."*

Imam Saadiq (A) is reported as saying: *'The faithful son of Adam[13] will be summoned for the reckoning and the Qur'an will go before him in the most beautiful of aspects and say: 'O Lord, I am the Qur'an and this is your faithful servant who used to tire himself by reciting me and spend long nights reading me and his eyes would stream when he spent the nights in prayer, so please him as he has pleased me.' Allah Almighty will say: 'Open your right hand, then he will fill it with the pleasure of Allah Almighty and he will fill his left hand with the mercy of Allah then he will be told: 'This garden of Paradise is open to you so recite and ascend and for every verse he recites he will ascend a station.'*

Imam Saadiq (A) is reported as saying: *'The believer should not die before learning the Qur'an or be in the process of learning it.'*

The Messenger of Allah (S) is reported as saying: *'Allah does not punish the heart which is a vessel for the Qur'an.'*

The Messenger of Allah (S) is reported as saying: *'The best of you is the one who learns the Qur'an and teaches it.'*

In one of his speeches contained in the book Nahj-ul-Balagha, Imam Ali (A) says: *'Learn Ye the Qur'an for it is the best of speech and study it for it is the springtime of the heart. Seek cure by its light for it heals the breast, and make your reading of it beautiful for it is the most beneficial of narratives. The learned man who acts without using his knowledge is as the ignorant, confused man who will never awake from his ignorance, in fact the case against him is greater and loss is more incumbent upon him, and in the sight of Allah he is the most blameworthy.*

The Messenger of Allah (S) is reported as saying: *'Allah will crown the parents of the one who teaches his child the Qur'an with a kingly crown and clothe them in robes the like of which has never been seen before.'*

The Messenger of Allah (S) is reported as saying: *'The people of the Qur'an are the people of Allah and His elect.'*

---

[13] Son of Adam is an expression meaning an individual.

The Messenger of Allah (S) is reported as saying: *'The best worship is the recitation of the Qur'an.'*

The Imam (A) said: *"The Qur'an is riches, there are no riches without knowledge of it and no poverty after knowledge of it."*

The Messenger of Allah is reported as saying: *"The nobles of my nation are those who bear the Qur'an (in their hearts), and the people of the night (who worship Allah during the hours of darkness)."*

The Messenger of Allah (S) also said: *"This Qur'an is the etiquette of Allah so learn his etiquette as much as you can."* He also said: *"This Qur'an is the rope of Allah and is the elucidating light, and the beneficial cure . . . and the stronghold for those who adhere to it and salvation for those who follow it."*

The Messenger of Allah (S) also said: *"Whoever reads the Qur'an in order to learn it by heart, Allah will allow him to enter the garden and his intercession will be accepted for ten of his family who had deserved the fire."*

The Imam (A) is reported as saying: *"The bearers of the Qur'an in this world are the wise men of the people of paradise on the day of resurrection."*

Also related from 'Ali (A) is that he said: *"If the teacher says to his pupil: Say: 'In the Name of Allah The Beneficent The Merciful.' And the pupil says: 'In The Name of Allah The Beneficent The Merciful.' Then Allah will give absolution to them both and to the pupil's parents."*

Respecting the Holy Qur'an

On the Obligation of Respecting the Holy Qur'an and following Its Guidance and the Unlawfulness of Disrespecting of It.

Ishaq Ibn Ghalib narrates from Imam Saadiq, (A), who said, *"On the day of judgement when all people are brought back to life at one place, a person will appear in such a beautiful form that no one would have ever seen such beauty before. The people will look at the individual, who is in fact the Qur'an, and will say that he is from our people but he has the best form that we have ever seen. This individual goes to the Divine throne and stands to its right. The Lord*

47

Almighty then will say to the Qur'an, "I swear by My Majesty, Greatness and Highness that I shall honour those who have honoured and respected you and disgrace those who disrespected you."

Abil Jarood has narrated from Imam Baaqir (A) who has narrated from the holy Prophet who has said, *"On the day of judgement I will be the first to come to the presence of Allah with the holy Qur'an and my family and then my followers. Then I will ask them about how they treated my family and the holy Qur'an."*

The holy Prophet (S) said, *"One who reads the holy Qur'an and then thinks that someone else has received a better reward, such person has belittled what Allah has made great and has considered great what Allah has belittled."*

Talha ibn Zayd has narrated from Imam Saadiq (A) who said, *"In this Qur'an is the torch of guidance and light for the darkness. Those who seek its light they will have their sight brightened and will find their eyes opened in the light. Thinking is life for the intelligent hearts just as one who finds light to walk in the darkness."*

Soma'a has narrated from Imam Saadiq (A) who has said, *"One who reads the holy Qur'an should pray to Allah for salvation, protection from Hell fire and wish for the best whenever one would read a verse of the Qur'an that contains some warning or prayers."*

Al-Sakooni has narrated from Imam Saadiq (A) who has narrated from his father and the holy Prophet who said, *"When confusion will surround you like a dark night, you must seek guidance from the holy Qur'an, because its intercession will not be declined and its testimony will be held true. Whoever will take it as his leader it will lead him to Paradise and whoever ignores it and puts it behind himself it will drive him into Hell. The holy Qur'an guides to the best path and it is a book in which is explanation, exposition, and learning. It is decisive and not in jest. It has an outside and an inside, its exterior is judgement, and its interior is knowledge, its outer manifestation is elegant and its inner meanings are deep. It has stars and upon its stars are more stars. Its marvels are without number, and its wonders never cease. It is the lanterns of guidance, and the lighthouse of wisdom, and the guide to knowledge for one who seeks the truth. One, thus, must open his heart in the light and let his eyes see the fact. The holy Qur'an saves one from destruction and frees one from entanglement. Thinking gives life to one who is alert-hearted just as light is for one who needs light to walk in the dark. You must seek your salvation in the best form and stop waiting."*

Imam Saadiq has narrated from Imam Ali, (A), who said in a long statement about the pious people, *"At night they stand up (for prayer) and read and recite the holy Qur'an one part after another. They make their souls to feel sad and reading the holy Qur'an makes their sadness increase. They weep for the sins (they have committed) and the pains of the cuts in their wounded feelings. Whenever they come across a passage of the holy Qur'an that speaks of warnings to mankind they open wide the ears of their hearts to them, their hairs standing on end, their hearts frightened and they imagine the roaring and pounding of the flames of the Hell fire striking against their ears. Whenever they come across a verses of the holy Qur'an that speaks of good news and encouragements they incline on them with hope and their souls filled with delight of reaching such goals."*

Imam Baaqir, (A), said: The Commander of the Faithful, (A), said: *"Shall I inform you about the true religious scholar? He is one who does not invoke in the people a despair of the mercy of Allah, nor does he invoke in them a sense of security from the punishment of Allah. He does not give licence to disobey Allah and does not neglect the Qur'an seeking other than it. Indeed there is no good in a knowledge in which there is not a deep understanding, nor is there any good in a recital of the Qur'an in which there is no pondering, nor is there any good in an act of worship in which there is no heartfelt comprehension."*

Memorising, Learning, and Teaching the Holy Qur'an

The Messenger of Allah is reported as saying: *"The people of the Qur'an have reached the highest degree of all the children of Adam, apart from the prophets and messengers. Therefore do not deny them their rights for they have from Allah The Almighty a lofty station."*

The Messenger of Allah (S) is reported as saying: *"The nobles of my nation are those who bear the Qur'an (in their hearts) (uphold the Qur'an), and the people of the night (who worship Allah during the hours of darkness)."*

The Messenger of Allah is reported as saying: *"The followers of holy Qur'an are the people with best knowledge of the truth in Paradise."*

Imam Hassan al-Askari (A) has said in his commentary of the holy Qur'an quoting his grand father, the holy Prophet (S), *"The upholders of the holy Qur'an are specially favoured with the mercy of Allah, they are clothed from the light of Allah, are taught the words of Allah and have been drawn near to Allah. Whoever loves them has loved Allah and whoever is hostile to them is hostile to Allah. Allah repels from one who listens to the holy Qur'an the worldly misfortunes and repels the misfortunes of the life hereafter from the one who recites the holy Qur'an. I swear by the One in Whose hands is Muhammad's soul, that reward for the listening, with faith, to the holy Qur'an being recited will be greater than a lot of gold spent for a good cause and the reward for reciting the holy Qur'an, with faith, will be greater than whatever is between the Throne and below the centre of the earth."*

Fuzayl Ibn Yasar has narrated from Imam Saadiq (A) who has said, *"One who memorizes the holy Qur'an and lives according to its guidance will have equal ranks with the honourable and virtuous Divine ambassadors."*

It is narrated from Imam Saadiq (A) who said, *"One who memorizes the holy Qur'an with difficulty, because of weaker memory, receives twice as much reward."*

Related from Imam Saadiq (A) who said: *'If one reads the Qur'an in his youth as a true believer, the Qur'an mingles with and becomes a part of his flesh and blood, and Allah places him alongside the pious and noble ambassadors, and on the day of resurrection the Qur'an will be a witness in his favour saying: 'O Lord, every doer of deeds has received the reward for his deeds except for him whose work was with me, so let him have the noblest of your gifts. Then Allah Almighty will clothe him in two of the robes of Paradise and the crown of honour will be placed upon his head. Then the Qur'an will be asked: 'Is this to your satisfaction?' And the Qur'an will answer: 'O Lord I desire for him something better than this.' So he will be given security in his right hand and everlasting life in his left then he will be ushered into Paradise and will be told: 'Recite a verse and for every verse ascend a station.' Then the Qur'an will be asked: 'Have We treated him to your satisfaction?' The Qur'an will answer 'Yes.'*

(The narrator said): *'Whoever recites a great amount of the Qur'an and underwent hardship due to the difficulty of memorisation will be given by Allah this twice over.'*

Aban Ibn Taghlib has narrated from Imam Saadiq (A) who said, *"A person who has both the holy Qur'an and faith his case is like citron with nice taste and aroma and the case of those who do not have the holy Qur'an nor faith is like colocynth which is bitter and has no good aroma."*

Fuzayl Ibn Yasar has narrated from the Imam Saadiq (A) who has narrated from the holy Prophet who said, *"Learn the holy Qur'an; on the day of judgement it will come to his friends in the form of a most beautiful young person of pale complexion and will speak to his friend saying, "I am the Qur'an for which you kept so often awake and endured thirst during the heat of midday, dried up your mouth and let your tears flow, I have good news for you. The man will receive a crown and peace will be placed on his right hand and eternal life in Paradise in his left hand and he will be dressed with two dresses of Paradise and then he will be told, "recite and rise." For each verse that he recites he will ascend one degree and his parents, if they are of the believers, each will receive two dresses of Paradise and they will be told that this is because of your teaching your child the holy Qur'an."*

Amir-ul-Mu'minin (A) is reported as saying: *"Allah, seeing people of the earth knowingly committing sins, decides to punish them all, but when He finds the old people going for prayer and the children learning the holy Qur'an, He then treats them with His mercy and postpones the punishment."*

Reverence of the Bearers of the Holy Qur'an

Imam Saadiq (A) has reported the holy Prophet, (S), as saying, *"The bearers and upholders of the Qur'an are the most entitled to be submissive to Allah in public and in private and they the most entitled to observe prayer and fasting in public and in private, and then the Prophet loudly said, "O upholders of the holy Qur'an, be humble by the holy Qur'an, Allah will uplift you and do not be malcontent or else Allah will bring you low. Upholders of the holy Qur'an, if you did observe proper manners in your relations with the holy Qur'an,*

Allah will make it a beauty for you. Let not such manners only be superficial to please people because Allah will then disgrace you. One who completes reading the holy Qur'an it will be just like incorporating prophet-hood within him, but only that Divine revelation does not come to him. One who upholds the holy Qur'an (by learning, understanding and following its guidance) he will not insult or respond in bad manners to those who do so and does not respond likewise to those who treat him with anger and, instead he forgives and ignores, pardons and endures for the sake of his respect towards the holy Qur'an. If one is fortunate to have the holy Qur'an and thinks someone else has some thing better than what he has, he certainly has revered what Allah has belittled and has belittled what Allah has revered."

Imam Baaqir (A) has said, *"The readers of the holy Qur'an are of three kinds: there is one who takes the holy Qur'an as a means of investments to attract the kings and dominate people. There is one who learns the letters of holy Qur'an but looses its laws and guidance and preserves just its form. May Allah let not the number of such people of the carriers of the holy Qur'an increase! There is one who reads the holy Qur'an and holds it to be the medicine for the ills of his heart. He keeps awake at night and endures thirst in the heat of the midday and he stands up with the holy Qur'an in his mosques and leaves his bed empty at night for prayer with the holy Qur'an. Through these people Allah repels misfortunes and changes the enemies, and through these people Allah sends down rain from the skies. I swear by Allah that such readers of Qur'an are more precious than red sulphur (the fountains of eternal life)."*

The Messenger of Allah (S) is reported as saying, *"If one reads the holy Qur'an and then drinks some thing unlawful or gets indulged in love of the worldly things, he becomes subject to the wrath of Allah unless he repents and if he dies without repenting, without any shred of doubt, on the day of judgement he will remain confound for ever."*

The Messenger of Allah (S) is reported as saying, *"If two groups of people in my followers behave properly the whole community of my followers will behave properly, and if these two groups are corrupt, the whole community will be corrupted; they are the readers of the holy Qur'an and the rulers."*

The Messenger of Allah (S) is reported as saying, *"One who learns the holy Qur'an and does not follow its guidance and instead prefers to love the worldly things and its attractiveness, he becomes subject to the wrath of Allah and he would be of the same rank as Jews and Christians who threw the Book of Allah behind their backs. One who reads the holy Qur'an using it as a means for the worldly gains and reputation, he, with his face without any flesh on it, will meet Allah on the day of judgement. And the holy Qur'an will push him into the Hell wherein he will fall with all those who will fall therein. One who reads the holy Qur'an and does not act according to its guidance he will be brought back to life on the day of judgement unable to see things and he will say, "Lord, why have you brought me back to life blind while in the world I was seeing things? Allah will say, "because Our signs came to you but you forgot all about them and thus, We have forgotten you today and the angels will be ordered to take him to Hell. One who reads the holy Qur'an in order to please Allah and to understand religion, his share of rewards will be equal to the rewards of all the angels, the prophets, and the messengers. One who reads the holy Qur'an in order to show off others and for the sake of worldly fame or to seek some kind of superiority over the people and boast before the scholars and make worldly gains, on the day of judgement Allah will scatter his bones and no one's sufferings will be more severe than his and there will be no suffering left with which he will not be punished because of severity of Allah's wrath against him. One who learns the holy Qur'an and is humble in knowledge and teaches the servants of Allah for Allah's rewards no one in Paradise will have more rewards then him or of higher ranks and there no rewards or degrees of excellence will be left in Paradise which he will not enjoy."*

The Messenger of Allah (S) is reported as saying, *"In Hell there is a valley and because of the severity of the sufferings therein the people of Hell cry for help seventy times every day and that will be the place for the wine drinkers and those who give up their prayers from my followers."*

It is narrated from Amir-ul-Mu'minin, Imam Ali, (A) who said, *"One who accepts Islam voluntarily and reads the holy Qur'an in its verbal sense, he will deserve a wage of two hundred Dinars per year from the Muslim treasury and if he is denied it in this world, on the day of judgement he will receive full compensation when he would most urgently need it."*

Frequent Reading of the Holy Qur'an

Mo'awiya Ibn Ammar narrates from Imam Saadiq, (A), who said about the will of the holy Prophet to Imam Ali, (A), *"You must read the holy Qur'an in all circumstances."*

Zuhri has said, I asked Imam Zayn-ul-Abidin (A), *"Which deed is more virtuous?"* He said, *"opening the holy Qur'an and reading to the end and whenever coming to the beginning of the holy Qur'an read it all the way to the end."*

Hafs has said, "I heard Imam Mussa al-Kaadhem (A), saying, *"The degrees of ranks in Paradise are equal to the number of the verses of holy Qur'an. One is told to read a verse and ascend one degree higher and so one would do."*

Abdullah Ibn Sulayman has narrated from Imam Baaqir, (A) who has said, *"Whoever reads the holy Qur'an in his prayer standing Allah will write for him for each letter one hundred virtue and for one who reads from the holy Qur'an in sitting position Allah will write fifty virtue for each letter read. One who reads the holy Qur'an in a state other then during one's prayer, Allah will write for him ten virtues for each letter."*

Bashir Ibn Ghalib al-Asadi has narrated from Imam Hussain, (A), who has said, *"Whoever reads from the holy Qur'an in his prayer in a standing position, Allah will write for him one hundred virtue for each letter and if one reads from the holy Qur'an in the conditions other than during prayer, Allah will write for him ten virtues for each letter, and if one listens to when the holy Qur'an is read, Allah will reward him for each letter one virtue. If one completes reading the holy Qur'an at night, the angles will pray for him until morning, and if he completes during the day the angles will pray for him until night and his prayers will be accepted and this will be better for him than all that is between the heavens and earth."* I said, *"this much for the reader of the holy Qur'an? What about one who does not read the holy Qur'an?"* He said, *"Allah is generous and glorious and kind whatever one would read from the holy Qur'an Allah will reward him accordingly."*

Muhammad Ibn Bashir narrates from Imam Zayn ul-Abidin, (A), and this Hadith is narrated from Imam Saadiq, (A), who said, *"One who just listens to the holy Qur'an being read, for every letter Allah will give him the reward for one good deed, deletes one of his bad deeds and raises him one degree higher. One who reads the holy Qur'an by looking at it but not in the state of prayer, Allah will write for him the reward for one good deed for each letter, deletes one of his bad deeds and raises him one degree higher. One who learns one pronounced letter from the holy Qur'an, Allah will write for him the reward for ten good deeds, delete ten of his bad deeds and raise him ten degrees higher."* The Imam said, *"I do not say for each verse, but I say for each letter, like B, T. etc."* The Imam said, *"One who reads from the holy Qur'an in his prayers while sitting, Allah gives him the reward of fifty good deeds for each letter, deletes fifty of his bad deeds and raises him fifty degrees higher. One who reads from the holy Qur'an in his prayer while standing, Allah gives him the reward for one hundred good deeds, deletes one hundred of his bad deeds and raises him one hundred degree higher. One who reads the holy Qur'an completely, his prayer will be heard sooner or latter."* I asked the Imam, *"Sir, all of the holy Qur'an?"* He said, *"yes, all of the holy Qur'an."*

Ishaq Ibn Ammar has narrated from Imam Saadiq (A) who said, *"One who reads one hundred verses of the holy Qur'an in his prayer during the night, Allah will write for him the reward for worshipping for the whole night. One who reads two hundred verses of the holy Qur'an in a condition other than the state of prayer, Allah will write for him on the protected tablet one 'Quintal of good deeds' and a Quintal is equal to one thousand two hundred measure and each measure is bigger than the mountain of Ohod."*

Anas narrates from the holy Prophet (S) who said, *"One who reads one hundred verses of the holy Qur'an his name will not be written among the names of the people unconcerned (about faith) and one who reads two hundred verses from the holy Qur'an, his name will be written among the names of those who worship during the night and one who reads three hundred verses from the holy Qur'an, the holy Qur'an will not protest against him, meaning that one who has memorized that much from the holy Qur'an, as it is commonly said, "the boy has read the holy Qur'an meaning that he has memorized that much."*

Imam Hassan al-Askary (A) has narrated from his forefathers who said, *"The Opening Surah of the holy Qur'an in terms of virtue is better than all the treasuries of the throne. Whoever reads with faith in love of the family of the Prophet, Allah will give him for each letter one good deed's reward and each of such good deed would be better for him than the whole world and all that it contains of all kinds of properties and good things and one who listens to this Surah being recited he too will receive the same amount of reward as that of the one who just read it, thus, you should read it as much as you could."*

It is narrated from the holy Prophet, (S), who said, *"This Qur'an is the rope of Allah and it is His illuminating light and useful cure. You must read it; Allah will give you the reward for ten good deeds for each letter that you would read. I do not say that for 'ALM' is ten, but in fact, for 'A' is ten and for 'L' is ten and for 'M' is ten."*

It is narrated from the holy Prophet, (S), who said, *"The companion (bearer) of the holy Qur'an will be told, "read from the holy Qur'an and ascend higher and higher and recite by the good tune that you would recited in the world before this; your final destination will be the last verse of the holy Qur'an that you would recite."*

The holy Prophet (S) has said, *"One who reads the holy Qur'an it would be as if he has incorporated the prophet-hood within himself except that Divine revelation will not come to him."*

Bakr Ibn Abdullah has said that once Omar come to the holy Prophet, (S) and said, *"O Holy Prophet, you have very strong fever."* The holy Prophet, (S) said, *"it did not stop me last night from reading thirty Surahs of the holy Qur'an, of which seven were of the long Surahs."* Omar then said, *"holy Prophet, Allah has already forgiven your past and future sins[14] and you still work so hard."* The holy Prophet (S) replied, *"Shouldn't I be a thankful servant?"*

---

[14] The Prophet (S) never committed any sins, and the above is a quote form the Qur'an where Allah addresses the Prophet (S) as such, but this is an indirect address to the Muslims and it is not meant to be the Prophet (S).

Ya'qub al-Ahmar has narrated from Imam Saadiq (A) who said, *"Master, I had learned the holy Qur'an but now I have forgotten some of it. Would you please, pray for me to Allah to help me learn it again?"* Upon this the Imam seemed shocked and said, *"May Allah and all of us help you learn the holy Qur'an again and we are about ten people."* Then he said, *"If one knew one Surah of the holy Qur'an and then leaves it alone (forgets it). On the day of judgement that Surah will come to him in the best form and will greet him and the man will ask, "who are you?"* It will say, *"I am Surah so-and-so of the holy Qur'an which you forgot me. If you had not forgot me, I would have taken you with me to this high rank."* The Imam then said, *"You must be very careful about the holy Qur'an."*

Abu Basir has narrated from Imam Saadiq, (A), who said, *"If one forgets a Surah of the holy Qur'an that he had memorized, on the day of judgement that Surah will come to him in the best form and with a high rank in Paradise and when the man sees it, he asks, "what are you? How beautiful you are. I wish you belonged to me."* The Surah of the holy Qur'an will say, *"Do you not know me? I am Surah so and so of the holy Qur'an had you not forgotten me; I could have taken you to this high position."*

Ya'qub al- Ahmar said, *"I said to Imam Saadiq, (A), "there is a lot of debts on me and I am about to forget the holy Qur'an."* The Imam, (A), said, *"The Qur'an! The Qur'an! On the day of judgement the Surah and the verses of the holy Qur'an will come ascend one thousand degrees in Paradise then and say, "If you had not forgotten me I would have taken you today to such and such high ranks in Paradise."*

Ya'qub al-Ahmar has said, "I said to Imam Saadiq, (A), *"Master, I am facing such problems, and difficulties that I am forgetting so many good things even some of the holy Qur'an."* The Imam was shocked and said, *"If a man forgets a Surah of the holy Qur'an on the day of judgement that Surah will come to him with a certain rank and greets him and the man asks, "Who are you? The Surah of the holy Qur'an will say, "I am Surah so and so of the holy Qur'an which you forgot, and I wish you had not have forgotten me, so that today I could have taken you to such and such high ranks and it will point to a certain rank."* The Imam then said, *"You must be very careful about the holy Qur'an. Some people learn the holy Qur'an so that others would call him a very good reciter of the holy Qur'an. Some people learn the holy Qur'an so that others would praise him for very good tune of reciting the holy Qur'an and there is nothing good in all of this. Some people learn the holy Qur'an and all night reading and contemplating the holy Qur'an, and during the day too, and they do not care whether others know his learning the holy Qur'an or not."*

Saed ibn Abdullah al-A'raj has said, *"I asked Imam Saadiq about a person who reads the holy Qur'an and then forgets it, reads it and then forgets it again, will there be any blame against him?"* The Imam said, *"no."*

Hussain Ibn Zayd has narrated from Imam Saadiq, (A), who has narrated from the holy Prophet, (S), who said, *"Whoever learns the holy Qur'an and then forgets it, he will meet Allah on the day of judgement tied up in chains and for each verse that he has forgotten Allah will send to him a snake that will stay with him in Hell until Allah forgives him."*[15]

Preparation for Reading the Holy Qur'an

Muhammad Ibn Fuzayl has said that I said to Imam Saadiq, (A), *"On occasions when I am reading the holy Qur'an, I need to use the rest room. I come back after I have washed myself and my hands and continue reading the holy Qur'an. Is this OK?"* The Imam said, *"no, (should not start reading the holy Qur'an) until you have formal 'Wudhu' purification."*

The author of al-Khisal narrates from Imam Ali, (A), who said, *"One must not read the holy Qur'an without formal purification (Wudhu)."*

Ahmad Ibn Fahd has said in 'Oddat-ul-Daa'i that Imam Ali, (A), has said, *"For every letter that one reads of the holy Qur'an in his prayer in a standing position Allah will give the reward for one hundred good deeds, fifty for each letter if one reads them in his prayers in a sitting condition and the reward of twenty good deeds if one reads them with formal purification but not in the state of prayer and the reward of ten good deeds if one reads them without formal*

---

[15] The *"forgetting"* of the verse means to abandon and ignore the laws and guidance of the holy Qur'an.

purification. I do not say that 'ALMR' as one, but in fact, (A) (L) (M) (R) for each letter there will be ten rewards."

It is narrated from Imam Hassan al-Askari, (A), who has said in his commentary of the holy Qur'an, *"The order of Allah that requires one to seek refuge in Allah before starting to read the holy Qur'an, is to say, "I seek refuge in Allah, Who listens and is Omniscient, from the Satan, the condemned." Amir-ul-Mu'minin has said, "I seek refuge in Allah, means I protect my self from Satan through Allah." Seeking refuge in Allah means to follow the order of Allah that says, "Whenever you read the holy Qur'an, seek refuge in Allah from Satan, the condemned. Whoever disciplines himself with Allah's discipline it will lead him to eternal betterment. Then he mentioned the long Hadith from the holy Prophet, (S), in which he said, "if you want not to be harmed by the evils of Satan, you should say every morning, "I seek refuge in Allah from Satan, condemned. Allah will give you protection against their evil deeds."*

Reciting the Holy Qur'an Anywhere and Anytime

Imam Saadiq, (A), is quoted as saying, *"The holy Qur'an is the covenant between Allah and His creatures. A Muslim must look into his covenant and read at least fifty verses from it every day."*

Zuhri has said, Imam Zayn al-Aabedeen, (A) said, *"Verses of the holy Qur'an are treasures, and whenever a treasure is opened one should look into it to find what there is in it."*

Imam Ali Redha, (A), is quoted as saying, *"Every day after the morning prayer one must read (at least) fifty verses of the holy Qur'an."*

Imam Saadiq, (A), said, *"When a Muslim reads from the holy Qur'an in his house, that house will shine to those in heaven just as stars from heavens shine to us on earth."*

Imam Saadiq quoted from Amir-ul-Mu'minin, Ali, (A), who said, *"A house in which the holy Qur'an is read and Allah is mentioned often, its blessings increase, the angels come to it, Satans move out of it and it will shine to those in heavens as stars shine to us from the heavens. A house in which the holy Qur'an is not read and Allah is not mentioned, its blessings decrease, the angels move out and Satans move in."*

Imam Saadiq, peace be up on them, is quoted as saying *"My father would call us together and would order us to say Thikr until sunrise and then would order those of us who could read to read from the holy Qur'an and to those who could not read, he would order them to say Thikr. The house in which the holy Qur'an is read and Allah is mentioned, blessings therein increase."*

The holy Prophet, (S), is quoted as saying, *"Light up your houses by reading from the holy Qur'an and do not turn them into your graves as the Jews and Christians had done; they would pray in their Synagogue and Churches and had ignored their houses. The house in which holy Qur'an is read often and Allah's holy names are mentioned, blessings therein increase, their people prosper and they shine to those in heavens as the stars from heavens shine to earth."*

Imam Ali al-Redha (A) has narrated from the holy Prophet (S) who said, *"Set for your house a share from the holy Qur'an; for the house in which the Qur'an is recited brings ease, and plenty for those who dwell in it and if the Qur'an is not recited in it then it will become difficult for the household and they will be in need."*

Imam Saadiq, (A), said, *"What stops a man, when he comes back home from work, from reading one Surah of the holy Qur'an before he goes to sleep? For he will be accredited with ten good deeds, and also ten foul deeds will be erased for each verse that he reads."*

Imam Saadiq has narrated from the holy Prophet, peace be up on them, who said, *"One who reads ten verses of the holy Qur'an each night his name will not be written among the names of those who do not care much about (religion) and one who reads fifty verses of the holy Qur'an each night, his name will be written with the names of those who remember Allah, one who reads one hundred verses of the holy Qur'an every night, his name will be written with the name of the worshippers, one who reads two hundred verses of the holy Qur'an, his name will be written with those who are submissive, before Allah, one who reads thee hundred verses, his name will be written with the victorious ones, one who reads five hundred verses, his name will be written with the hard working ones for the cause of Allah, and one who reads one thousand verses of the holy Qur'an, one Quintar will be written for him and a Quintar is fifteen thousand (or fifty thousand) Mithqual of gold and a Mithqual is twenty Quirat, the smallest of which is equal to the size of the mountain of Ohod and the biggest of them is the size of the space between heaven and earth."*

Abi Hamza al-Thamali has narrated from Imam Baaqir, (A), who has said, *"One who reads all of the holy Qur'an in Mecca in one week or before a week or more than a week and completes it on Friday, Allah will write for him the reward of all the good deeds that may have taken place since the first in this world Friday to the last Friday that will come in this world and the same would be the case if reading is completed in other days."*

Jabir (al-Ansari) has narrated from Imam Baaqir, (A), who said, *"For every thing there is spring. The spring for the holy Qur'an is the month of Ramadan."*

Reciting the Holy Qur'an from a Copy

Imam Saadiq, (A), said, *"One who recites the holy Qur'an from a copy of the holy Qur'an he will enjoy his eye-sight and lighten the burden of his parents even if they were not be believers."*

It is narrated from the holy Prophet (S) who said, *"There is nothing more difficult for the Satan (to tackle) than someone's reading of the holy Qur'an from a copy (of the Qur'an)."*

Ishaq ibn Ammar said, *"I asked Imam Saadiq, (A), 'Sir, I have learnt the holy Qur'an by heart. Which would be more rewarding, reciting the Qur'an from memory, or from a copy of the holy book?"* The Imam, (A), said, *"There is more reward for reading from a copy of the holy book (than from reciting it from memory). Don't you know that looking at the holy Qur'an is an act of worship?"*

It is narrated from Abu Tharr who narrated from the holy Prophet, (S) who said, *"Looking at Ali ibn Abi Talib is an act of worship, looking at one's parents affectionately and kindly is an act of worship, looking at the holy Qur'an is an act of worship and looking at the holy Ka'abah is an act of worship."*

Imam Saadiq, (A), who has narrated from his father who said, *"I admire that there be a copy of the holy Qur'an in the house with which Allah would repel the Satan."*

Imam Saadiq, (A), said, *"Three things will complain to Allah, the Most Glorious: a mosque which is damaged and the people of that mosque do not pray in it, a scholar among the ignorant people and the holy Qur'an covered dust which no one reads."*

Manners of Reading and Listening to the Holy Qur'an . . .

Abdullah Ibn Sulayman has said, *"I asked Imam Saadiq, (A), about Allah's saying, "read the holy Qur'an distinctly",* the Imam said, that Amir-ul-Mu'minin Imam Ali, (A) has said, *"read clearly, not deliriously like it is done in reciting poetry, nor recite it scattered like pieces of pebbles but strike with it your hardened hearts and none of you should think it most important to finish the Surah (quickly)."*

Imam Saadiq, (A) said, *"Read the holy Qur'an in Arabic clearly and correctly, it is in Arabic that means clear."*

Imam Saadiq, (A) said, *"It is undesirable to read the whole Surah of 'Ikhlas', or 'Unity of Allah', in one breath, without a pause between the verses."*

Abi Bask has narrated from Imam Saadiq, (A), who said about Allah's saying in the holy Qur'an *'recite the holy Qur'an distinctly'*, *"It means that you should pause, as and when punctuation rules require and recite in a nice tune."*

It is narrated from Umm Salamah who has said, *"The holy Prophet, (S), would read the holy Qur'an pausing between the verses."*

Imam Saadiq, (A), said, *"The holy Qur'an is revealed in serenity and concerned and it should be read in the same way."*

Abdullah Ibn Sinan has narrated from Imam Saadiq, (A), who said, *"Allah, the Most High told Moses, "whenever you stand before Me, stand as a humble poor person and when you read Torah to Me read it in a sad tune."*

It is narrated from Hafs who said, *"I never saw anyone more afraid about himself than Imam Mussa al-Kaadhem, (A), or anyone more hopeful (for Allah's mercy) than him. He would recite the holy Qur'an with sadness and it was as he was addressing someone."*

Imam Baaqir, (A), said, *"One who recites the Surah "Power" (97) of the holy Qur'an with a loud voice, he would be like one who has drawn his sword for the cause of Allah and one who reads it silently, he would be like one who is killed in the cause of Allah, and one reads it ten times an order is issued to delete one thousand of his sins."*

Mo'awiyah Ibn Ammar has said, *"I told Imam Saadiq, (A), "the man does not think that he has read anything from the holy Qur'an or prayers unless he says them loudly." The Imam, (A), said, "It does not matter. Imam Zayn al-Aabedeen, (A), would recite the holy Qur'an in the most pleasant tune and he would read it loudly such that every one in the house would hear him. Imam Baaqir, (A), had the best reciting tune and he would recite the holy Qur'an loudly during the night and whoever would pass by would stop to listen to his recitation."*

It is narrated from Abu Tharr who narrated from the holy Prophet, (S), who said in his will, *"Aba Tharr lower your voice when walking in a funeral procession, in combat and when hearing the recitation of the holy Qur'an."*

Abdullah Ibn Sinan has narrated from Imam Saadiq (A), who has narrated from the holy Prophet, (S), who said, *"Read the holy Qur'an in Arabic tune and voice and never recite it in the voice and tune of the sinful and people committing major sins; after me there will come people who twist their tune in reciting the holy Qur'an as the singers, mourners and the monks. It is not lawful to promote them; their hearts and the hearts of those who like their actions are turned upside down."*

Ali ibn Muhammad al-Nawfali has narrated from Imam Abi al-Hassan, (A), who said, *"When 'Fine reciting tunes' were mentioned before him, upon this he said, "Imam Zayn al-Aabedeen, (A), had a very fine reciting tune and whenever someone would pass by when he was reciting the holy Qur'an, the person would stop in astonishment because of the Imam's beautiful recitation."*

Abdullah ibn Sinan has narrated from the holy Prophet who said, *"For every thing there is some ornament, the ornament of reciting the holy Qur'an is fine recital tune."*

Imam Ali Redha, (A), said, *"The holy Prophet, (S), has said, "Recite the holy Qur'an in nice tunes because it gives beauty to the Qur'an."*

It is narrated from Jabir who said, *"I asked Imam Baaqir, (A), about a people who on hearing anything about the holy Qur'an or the reward about it get shocked to an extent that even if the hands or legs of one of them were amputated they would not notice."* The Imam, (A), said, *"Glory be to Allah. They were not told to behave as such. It is only serenity, soft heartedness, tears, fear and concern."*

Imam Saadiq, (A), was asked, *"When one reads from the holy Qur'an is it obligatory for others to keep silent and listen to it?"* The Imam replied, *"Yes, when the Qur'an is recited you must keep silent and listen to it."*

Imam Abi al-Hassan, (A), said, *"I asked him, "my father asked your grand father about reading the whole Qur'an in one night."* He said, *"every night."* Then he said, *"in the month of Ramadhan."* Your grand father asked him, *"in the month of Ramadhan."* My father said, *"yes, sir, in the month of Ramadhan if I could."* Then my father used to read the holy Qur'an forty times in the whole month of Ramadhan. Then I after my father would read the holy Qur'an some times more and some time less than him according to my timework, activities, and laziness. On 'Eid day after the month of Ramadhan, I would assign the reward for reading the holy Qur'an once for the holy Prophet, one Imam Ali, one for Lady Fatimah and one for each Imam until your self and I assigned the reward for reciting the holy Qur'an once for you from the time I am doing this. Will there be any thing for me in this?"* The Imam said, *"because of this, on the Day of Judgment, you will be with them."* Allah is great! I said: This (honour) is for me? The Imam, (A), said, *"yes"* three times.

Imam Saadiq (A) narrated that some youth from Ansar came to the holy Prophet, (S). He to them said, *"I want to read some thing to you whoever of you would weep, Paradise will be for him and then he recited the last verse of Surah thirty nine, "the disbelievers will be driven into Hell in groups..."* Every one wept except one young man who said, *"holy Prophet, I tried to weep but no tears came out."* The *holy Prophet, (A), said, "I repeat for you, if any one who would try to weep, Paradise will be for him." He repeated and people and the young man tried to weep and they all went to Paradise."*

It is narrated from Imam Ja'far Ibn Muhammad from his forefathers who have narrated from the holy Prophet, peace be up on them, who said, *"you must learn the holy Qur'an in Arabic and be careful about 'al-nabz', which means the letter 'Hamza'. Imam Saadiq said, "al-hamza in the Qur'an is an addition except the original al-hamza as in al-khabaa', Di' and Faddara'tum."*

Imam Saadiq, (A), said, *"Learn Arabic; it is the language of Allah in which He spoke to His creatures and talked to the people of the past."*

Imam al-Jawaad, (A), said, *"two people are never equal in religion or race but better among them in the sight of Allah is the well disciplined one among them." I said, "we can see their discipline in the eyes of the people in their activities in the society but how we would know his discipline in the sight of Allah?" The Imam said, "By his reading the holy Qur'an the way it was revealed, by his prayers without tunes; prayer with tunes are not raised to Allah."*

Imam Saadiq, (A), said, *"the holy Prophet has said, "A none Arab of my followers reads the holy Qur'an in his none Arabic way but the angels raise his reading in Arabic."*

THE SYSTEM OF ISLAM

There is no doubt that Islam has its own particular system and there also is no doubt that the Islamic system was working, whether when fully or partially implemented, for thirteen centuries until its downfall about half a century ago.

One also hears that the Islamic civilization was an exemplary one to a great degree, and that the Islamic System has sufficient solutions to world problems and if is brought back the world will become Paradise.

Then what is that system? Is it possible for an Islamic system to come back to life during the space and nuclear age? And how it would solve the problems if it did really take charge of the running of the affairs (of a state)?

These are questions worth answering . . . The Answers that will be given to such questions in this book may astonish the reader and he might think that we are talking of some Utopian city. The author is ready to meet the challenge of giving such answers and to present the proofs and evidences according to the teachings of Islam for such answers, and he would prove that it is quite possible for the system of Islam to come back to life. The author has written several books on this topic, both brief and detailed works and this discourse is a brief presentation in this respect.[16]

---

[16] For more details on the author's work in this particular field, see
"If Islam Were To Be Established", *"Islamic System of Government"*,
"Single Universal Islamic Government", *"Government in Islam, al-Fiqh series, vol. 99"*,
"The Islamic Government, al-Fiqh series, volumes 101-102", *"Politics, al-Fiqh series,*
volumes 105-106", *"Economics, al-Fiqh series, volumes 107-108"*, etc.

1. Politics

Question: Is there politics in Islam?

Answer: Yes, Islam has the best form of politics to bring order in the society.

Q. Is the Islamic system of government a republic or monarchist system?

A. It is neither republic nor monarchist in the conventional sense. It is a form of consultative and advisory government and it would be correct to call it democracy. There is no monarchist or heredity system of government in Islam.

Q. Who would be the head of the Islamic government?

A. He is a Muslim believer who has thorough expertise in Islam. He is proficient about the worldly affairs and is armed with the ability not to deviate from the standards of justice in all matters. Whoever possesses these qualities and the majority of people accept him, he can be the head of the government even if for fifty years. Whenever he looses any of these qualities he is removed from his position immediately. However, if the people would not agree with his leadership they have the right to change him and choose another individual who also possesses those qualities.

Q. Who chooses the Islamic head of government?

A. The majority of the people do.

Q. Are there elections, voting, parliament, and municipalities in the Islamic system?

A. Yes, it has all of these. The parliament is to apply and implement the general laws to whatever they are applicable but it is not for legislating tasks (outside the framework of Islamic laws).

Q. What are the duties and tasks of Islamic Government?

A. It upholds justice between people, inside and outside the country and pushes life forward to progress.

Q. What laws are adhered to in the Islamic government?

A. The laws that are derived from the Qur'an, traditions of the holy Prophet, consensus, and reason.

Q. Who gives these laws the final shape for practical purposes?

A. The scholars who specialise in the study of the Islamic laws and who do not deviate from the standards of justice who are expert in both religious and current affairs.

Q. Are there political parties in the Islamic system?

A. There is no problem with the existence of parties that are introductory to the parliament that enforces the laws, but there is no party that would work as an introduction to a parliament that is a legislative parliament; legislation is only in the hands of Allah, the Most High.

2. The Economy

Q. Is there any system of economy in Islam?

A. The best system the world has known.

Q. Is the system of economy in Islam capitalist, socialist, communist or distributive?

A. It is none of the above in the conventional sense.

Q. What is then the system of economy in Islam?

A. It allows private ownership, provided that earnings are not obtained by unlawful means and all income liabilities are paid.

Q. What are the government's sources of income?

A. The taxes that Islam has sanctioned.

Q. What are these taxes?

A. There are four taxes: *Khums*, *Zakat*, *Kheraj*, and *Jizyah*.

Q. Can you explain these taxes?

A.

Khums   The *Khums* of 20% levied is on untaxed, superfluous annual income from all forms of earnings. These earnings include earnings from the minerals, found treasures, pearls and other artefacts from the sea, the earnings that are mixed with unlawful earnings, the spoils of the battlefield and some sorts of land.

Zakat   *Zakat* rate ranges from 1% to 2.5% levied on sheep, cows, camels, gold, silver, raisins, date, barley, and wheat once over certain threshold.

Jizyah   *Jizyah* is the tax levied on non-Muslims living under the protection of the Islamic state.

Khiraj   *Khiraj* is the income from letting conquered land, if any, to farmers.

Q. Is there any banking system in Islam?

A. Yes there is, but without usury, and provided that all the banking laws also comply with Islamic laws. The expenses of its employees are met from various incomes of the bank and if they were not sufficient then the department of treasury would pay. [This is in the case of a government bank, where profit of the bank goes to treasury, hence when income not enough the treasury department covers the deficit.]

Q. Would the Islamic government take other taxes like those that people pay today?

A. No. The government has no right to seek any taxes other than the four mentioned. The government may, temporarily, need to seek extra taxes in exceptional emergency circumstances. Such cases will be considered on their own merit.

Q. What would the Islamic government do with the money it receives from public?

A. The government uses the *Bayt-ul-Maal* (the treasury department) to meet all the expenses of the Muslims. In addition, it will pay for the expenses of all the projects of reforms and developments in the country, help the needy to run their affairs so that there no destitute is left in the society, like helping people to get married, start a business, buy a house, treatment of illness, travelling for necessity or one is left without money while on a journey etc. if he could prove - in a simple way, like providing evidence or witness, or even swearing on oath - his needs, then the treasury would provide him assistance. In this way there will be no destitute left without help under the Islamic system of government.

Q. Will those four categories of taxes be enough for all such expenses?

A. It will be enough in addition to the government's other income from its tenements and possessions as well as natural resources such as oil etc.

Q. How it could be enough when we see today that all the big taxes still are not enough?

A. The number of government employees in the Islamic government will be small, because, in the Islamic government there is no need for many of the departments and their associated army of civil servants. Under an Islamic system of government, the public will do many of the jobs done by today's governments, and jobs left for the government to do will be done in a very little time and expense and in the simplest way. When there are just a few employees, and bureaucracy is reduced, the expenses will be reduced and there will be more money available.

Q. Is there any pension scheme in Islam?

A. If one is needy and not able to earn he receives help for what he needs, not a fixed amount, as it is in governments today otherwise there will be no such payments unless an establishment requires it.

3. The Army

Q. Does the Islamic system of government have an organised army?

A. Yes, it has an organised army in the best form.

Q. Is there compulsory draft system?

A. No. Serving in the Islamic army is voluntary except in an emergency situation.

Q. How would that work?

A. Those who would like to serve in the army may do so if they wish to stay in the army permanently and they would receive salary on that basis. The Islamic government would also arrange training opportunities for members of the public so that every one receives training and this would reduce the expenses for the army. In this members of the (territorial) army would remain near their families and places of their work. Every one will attend training courses every day for some hours and then go to their own work. When there is an attack on the country every one rises to defend the Islamic government.

Q. What is the Islamic opinion about the modern tools of warfare?

A. The Islamic system considers it necessary to manufacture and possess whatever tools required, as Allah, the Most High, has said, *"And make ready for them whatever you can of power."* The Qur'an, Public Estate (8): 60.

Q. What the Islamic government would do for the relatives of those killed in the battlefield?

A. If they are needy and not able to make their living the government will help them with whatever they may need and if they are not needy they will not receive anything unless there is a certain interest in helping them.

4. Freedoms

Q. Is there freedom in Islam?

A. Yes. Islam provides the best form of freedom. A freedom the world has not dreamed of even in the best of civilisations it has come across.

Q. What are the Islamic freedoms?

A. There are many forms of freedoms and we will only mention a few in the following:

1. Freedom in trade, in which every one can import or export goods and buy or sell without restrictions at all. There is no custom charges or tariffs and no conditions, however, the goods must be lawful for buying and selling and not things like liquor etc., and that there is no

unlawful interest involved or that the transaction is unlawful or the trading involves monopoly and that it does not constitute harm to the Islamic government.

2. Freedom in agriculture. One would be allowed to farm any amount of land and in any manner that he wants he would be entitled to it and there is no land reform in the conventional sense, in Islam. However, if the land is taken from the enemy by force by the government then the farmer has to pay a small amount of rent to the government, this rent is called Kheraj, and if the farmer is poor the government must help him out. One is allowed to farm as much land as he can, provided, this will not seize other people's opportunities. The government cannot demand for more taxes other than *Khums* and *Zakat* with all the conditions required.

3. Freedom in manufacturing and construction, one is allowed to develop the land in any way he wants and there will be no tariffs on such developments. The government has no right to make him pay even a single penny for the land or other things. Islam has said, "whoever develops the barren land it becomes his", except if the land has been taken forcibly by the government from the enemy in which case the developer would pay rent to the government. There is also freedom in all forms of manufacturing technology in every sense of the word except unlawful products.

4. Freedom in business and work, like hunting, mining, procurement of the permissible and doing all kinds of lawful businesses in whatever way one wants and the government will not ask for any taxes for the land etc., however, it is not permissible to do those businesses that are not lawful in Islam.

5. Freedom of travelling and residence; one may reside wherever he wants or travel to wherever he wants and there will be no condition required of him. There are no geographical borders (between Muslim countries) in Islam, no racial conditions, no discriminations due to colour or language etc. With this freedom there will be no identity cards, permits and passports and other things related to this except, for exceptional circumstances and the emergencies are only for the time needed.

6. Freedom of activities of all forms and shapes except those prohibited in Islam, which are just a few and, thus, no secret police

will be needed, besides the department for collecting information for the benefits of the government. There is freedom to speak, write, form organizations and corporations and publishing magazines, newspapers, setting up broadcasting stations etc.

Q. The issues mentioned here would require dismantling many of the government departments we see today.

A. That is correct. This is how an Islamic system of government would work. There would not be many government departments under an Islamic system of government, but just a few as mentioned before, and because of this, the number of government employees will reduce significantly and therefore the government will not need to levy massive taxes on the public to run its affairs.

5. The Justice System

Q. Is there a comprehensive judicial system in Islam?

A. Yes. A system of justice in the best form exists in Islam.

Q. How is the Islamic system of Justice?

A. The judge must be a man of Islamic faith, and a practicing Muslim who is expert in Islamic judicial laws. He will judge the cases without any fees, and he does not require formal applications for the hearing. One judge will look into all kinds of cases in order to issue the Islamic verdict for each case.

The criterion for the witness is that he must be a practicing Muslim. There are no formal protocols and bureaucracies in the Islamic judicial system, and therefore one judge used to be able to deal with all the cases of a town, such that there was no case unresolved.

Q. Where does the judge receive his salary?

A. He will be paid from *Bayt-ul-Maal* (or the department of treasury).

Q. What is the duty of a judge?

A. With the help of his assistants he would be involved in many tasks. He would supervise the affairs of charitable properties and religious endowments, the properties and affairs of individuals who are not independent, mentally or because of age etc., such as looking into the marital problems of such people and the management of their properties and wealth, i.e. he would safeguard their wealth and properties and return them to them when they are older or when they are fit to take charge of their affairs. He would supervise marriage, divorce, and certify contracts between parties, etc. He would also be involved in settling disputes among individuals and executing the penalties and punishments to be carried out.

Q. Is there any role for attorneys in the Islamic judicial system?

A. There will be no need for an extensive network of attorneys, since the affairs concerned run with ease and simplicity.

Q. What the government will do for the attorneys?

A. The system will provide them with other projects and activities that will be progressive and constructive and will pay them from the treasury to help them start another career.

6. Health

Q. Is there any health program in Islam?

A. Yes. It has the best of preventive and treatment system.

Q. How does this system work?

A. Islam, through general guidelines, provides the following three measures for the health care programs.

1. The preventive measures that help control the spread of disease:

(a) It prohibits getting involved in matters that cause disease, like alcohol, adultery, music, practices that bring anxieties, etc.

(b) By observing etiquette, traditions, and general discipline such as cleanliness, occasional blood-letting by cupping or venesection, personal hygiene, fasting, marriage, use of body creams, use of herbal treatment, manners of eating and drinking, etc.

2. Treatment of disease by means of proper medical and dietary procedures all of which are simple and easy. Such measures although may not be comprehensive but they would stop the disease especially at the outset of the disease. Detailed health care and dietary programs

are given in the "health guidelines" of the Holy Prophet and Imams, peace be up on them.

3. Supervision of the health care programs includes dose examinations of the physicians' treatment of the patients. The Islamic law holds a physician responsible for any misconduct, even though being an expert. This creates a strong sense of responsibility that makes the physician more observant when diagnosing and treating the disease, and prescribing medicine.

Q. Has medical knowledge not made a significant progress?

A. There is no doubt about progress in the medical science, however, the basic foundations that we have mentioned, which are the principle pillars of general health care, have been destroyed and thus we see mankind is afflicted with all sorts of diseases to the degree that the huge numbers of physicians and health care facilities are not enough to maintain the health of the general public. We remember that our forefathers had enjoyed good health until the last days of their lives and today we see that every household has one or more people suffering from a certain illness and many people suffer from one or several medical complications.

Q. What is the remedy then?

A. The Islamic health care program must be introduced, and as well as all the useful facilities of the new discoveries (of the health care programs today). This must be done so provided that all the Islamically unlawful issues associated with it are discarded. The way for the tried-and-tested herbal medical programs should be opened up so that both methods merge, and in this way mankind will be saved from the grip of diseases.

7. Education

Q. Does Islam have any comprehensive educational program?

A. Yes, it has the best of educational programs.

Q. What are those programs?

A. Islam has made it compulsory for the Muslims, male and female, to acquire knowledge, and it provides the means for it, and it has made it compulsory for the government to support the educational program.

Q. Why then the Muslims are so behind?

A. They remained behind from the day they abandoned the Islamic teachings. At the time when the Muslims were adhering to its teachings they were much ahead in the field of education and there is no better proof for this than the western people's own acknowledgements of this fact. The number of books, libraries, schools, and educated people, with regards to those days facilities, much more than the books, libraries, schools and educated people today despite all the means and conditions available.

Q. Does Islam prohibit schools, newspapers, televisions, radios, and cinemas?

A. Islam prohibits unlawful, harmful and of evil temptations of such educational means if they would be free of such problems, Islam will be of the strong supporters of such educational means.

Q. What are the major differences between the Islamic educational programs and the conventional educational programs today?

A. The general difference is that Islam combines knowledge, faith, and virtue, while conventional educational programs ignore faith and virtue and instead has mixed atheistic and immoral ideas in it. Thus, knowledge, which is the best means for progress, peace, and security, has become a tool of degradation, destruction, and distress.

8. Peace

Q. Is Islam a religion of peace or a religion of war?

A. Islam is the religion of peace, as the holy Qur'an says, *"O believers, enter into peace completely."* The Heifer (2): 208. However, if any one would commit an act of aggression against people, or against the Muslims, Islam then defends itself to protect justice, truth and to repel the aggression.

Q. How Islam supports peace?

A. In Islam it is necessary to let peace prevail both internally and externally. Inside the country it abolishes crimes, outside the country it does not commit acts of aggression against any one, and it holds back the hands of the aggressors.

Q. How Islam would abolish crimes?

A. The causes behind committing crimes are: poverty, elements of evil temptations, ignorance, animosity, and sufferings etc. Islam fights against all of such elements until they are eliminated, and when they are eliminated, crimes will subsequently be abolished. A destitute person, for example, steals to survive, attractive women could lead to adultery, and liquors lead to crime. Ignorance causes transgression and animosity causes hurting others and murder. Family problems cause tribulation and crimes. Islam abolishes poverty, stops unlawful display of sexual beauty and liquors, provides education for all, removes the causes of animosity etc., and settles problems with easy judgments and quick decisions.

Q. How are the criminals punished in the Islamic system?

A. After abolishing the causes of crimes and providing a tranquil environment, Islam comes down with stern punishment up on the criminals. That is because he has committed them due to his meanness of nature and his deviation in the desires of his soul. With quick and stern punishment the environment is sterilized and crimes would not be repeated.

For example, four fingers of a thief are amputated, after all the conditions for such a verdict are present[17] of which one is for the destitute to have adequate and sufficient means of living, no one would contemplate stealing. For this reason, history shows that very few fingers were cut during the two centuries of the Islamic government.

Q. What would Islam do with the prisons?

A. Islam does not recognise any of the conventional, man-made laws. The only laws are the divine laws. Thus, many of the things called crimes today are not crimes according to Islam for anyone to be jailed for them. Whatever Islam considers a crime, like theft or fornication, it has set a certain quick punishments for them, like cutting the fingers

---

[17] There are more than forty preconditions, all of which must be met simultaneously before such a punishment may be implemented. See *"The Dynamics of Change for the Salvation of the Muslims"* pp 448-451.

and whipping. However, for a few crimes there is jail in Islam, like a delinquent in paying his due debts. Jail is what the judge asks an individual to keep the criminal in a room of his home, for example. Thus, there is no jail in the conventional sense in Islam at all. In the case of urgent needs jails are built in simple forms.

Q. How Islam will keep peace outside the country?

A. Islam does not allow transgression against any one at all. Whatever country would like to have peace, Islam also likes to have peace. The holy Qur'an says, *"If they incline to peace, incline to it too."* Public Estate (8): 61. If war is created, Islam deals with it in the most decent manners as history has recorded its uniqueness. Whatever country would commit aggression against Islam it will repel such acts of aggressions.

Q. How Islam will keep peace between the people and the government?

A. The government in Islam is the government of the people in the true sense of the word. What would people want other than the right to vote, self-sufficiency, education, freedom, security, health and virtue that Islam provides for them in the best form? This is why the good governments of the Muslims had lived for so long. It was because of the mutual love between the nation and the government. The leader did not need security forces and bodyguards to protect him against the people except in the case of emergency.

9. The Family

Q. What is Islam's view of marriage?

A. Marriage is permissible for the female after the age of nine with maturity and after the male's adulthood, which comes at the age of fifteen at which time getting married is very much recommended so that they would not fall in indecency.

Q. What are the duties of both spouses in family life?

A. The husband must provide all the expenses and satisfy her emotionally in accordance with the rules of law. The wife must obey the husband about going out of the house and her availability to the husband for emotional pleasures. It is not of the duties of women to work around the house. For marriage the consent of both the husband and wife is required. Divorce is in the hands of man alone unless specified otherwise in the marriage contract, when it will be in her hands too.

Q. What is Islam's view of women?

A. According to Islamic viewpoint, family life is incomplete without the hard work outside the house and tranquillity and work inside the house. Therefore, it has divided the matter: Man's share is outside and woman's share inside the house, thus, the house is the best place to grow and develop physically as well as intellectually and emotionally. Islamic wisdom views this that if women would start to undertake men's works it would necessitate to leave her works inside the house for men and this would be a waste of two abilities, waste of the noble emotions of women that is very vital for inside the house and waste of the work power of men required for the outside the house. Work is work except that if turned upside down it gives undesirable results. For this reason it is best for women to do works inside the house.

Q. Does Islam prohibit women from learning and working?

A. Never, Islam has not prohibited women from learning and work, it only has prohibited abusive and pervert manners and bedecking themselves in public. Islam also prohibits women from the kind of works that would be against their chastity and status.

Q. How does Islam view the family?

A. From the Islamic point of view it is necessary for women to have proper *Hijaab* as Allah has said, *"if you ask from them (women) (for an item) ask from behind a Hijaab"* and this reduces problems and strengthens the relations between the husband and wife and the family lives in an environment of love and serenity. *Hijaab* means that women must cover their hair and beauties.

Q. What is the Islamic view about boys and girl's mixing during different phases of life?

A. It is not permissible at all, whether it is during recreational times, at cinemas and swimming pools, at school, factories, social gatherings and clubs etc. From the Islamic point of view such mixing would lead to immorality which requires the system to take quick preventive measures against it, unless the mixing is out of necessity like those that take place during pilgrimage or Hajj.

Q. What is the Islamic view about polygamy?

A. It is permissible in Islam to have up to four wives, but it is obligatory to maintain justice among them. In this way the Islamic system solves the problems of unmarried and widows.

10. The Supplement

1. The Islamic society has a special characteristic that other societies today do not have. It enjoys the benefit of faith, which regulates the behaviour such that no other earthly system can ever do. And for this reason Islam gives a very sublime meaning to man while today's world speaks of man in terms of iron and machines. In an Islamic society many psychological and today's problems go away. Trust, love, and kindness to individuals and the society will increase.

2. Life, in all dimensions, will blossom under the Islamic system. Housing, farming, industrialization, expansion of trades and growth of wealth in an environment free of injustice, restrictions and conditions and a society free of sufferings and poverty. For this reason, developments, love of progress and trust in each other in the beginning of Islam were the norm, a fact that no one has experienced today, even though there is an abundance of means to improve standards of living.

3. It is imperative for everyone to do their best to re-establish the single universal Islamic government for all Muslims, and in the process Allah is the supporter.

On the Halal and Haram Conducts

This section lists some of the conducts that have been prescribed as *Haram* or forbidden, and *Halal* or permissible.

(A) List of Conducts Prohibited In Islam

Allah, the most High says in the holy Qur'an:

"Say (O Muhammad) "Come! I will recite to you what your Lord has forbidden to you."- *The Qur'an: The Cattle (6): 151.*

Just as it is compulsory for a Muslim to learn his or her (religious) *obligations* and act upon them, it is also compulsory for the Muslim to learn the *forbidden matters* and avoid them. Therefore we have listed here some of the prohibited matters that one may often come across in every day activities:

Beliefs

- Not to believe in Allah.
- To consider individuals or things as partners of Allah.
- To believe that Allah has children.
- Praying, prostrating or kneeling for something other than Allah.
- To consider oneself above the worship of Allah.
- To become unconcerned about the wrath of Allah.
- To abandon the practice of remembrance of Allah.
- To protest against Allah on fate and destination.
- Disputing with Allah, the prophets, and the Imams, peace be up on them.
- To cause difficulties for the Prophet, (S).
- Swearing to disassociate oneself from Allah, the prophets, the Imams and Islam.
- Lying against Allah, the Prophet, or Imams.

- To deny one of the principles of religion
- To deny any aspect of the holy Qur'an or the laws of *Shari'ah.*
- Blasphemy, especially, in the house of Allah.
- To become hopeless of the mercy of Allah.
- To deny the hereafter
- To deny miracles.

Shari'ah & Religion

- Not to comply with the laws of the Shari'ah.
- Not learning the basic principles of beliefs and the details of the rules of the religion.
- Not teaching the principles and rules of religion to those who are ignorant of them, when they are seen acting or practicing something, which is wrong.
- Innovating in (the laws and practices of) religion.
- Declaring the lawful as unlawful.
- Declaring the unlawful as lawful.
- Giving judgement not in accordance with Allah's orders.
- To rebel against the Imam, (the leader who is appointed by divine instructions).
- Denying what is due to Allah (e.g. *Khums, Zakat*).
- Refusing to pay religious taxes such as *Khums, Zakat,* or other obligatory dues.
- Delaying one's dues.
- Not exercising *Taqiyah* when in danger. [A Muslim must exercise all means within his disposal to protect his life when threatened. *Taqiyah* is not to disclose one's belief under certain severe circumstances in order to protect his life.]
- Migrating to places where one's religion would be endangered.
- Friendship with the enemies of religion in the absence of an urgent necessity.

- Swearing in general, especially towards Allah, the prophets, the Imams, Islam, Qur'an, and other sacred things.
- To mislead people away from the path of Allah.

Obligations

- Not practicing the principle of *"Enjoining Good and Forbidding Evil"*.
- To break an obligatory fast such as that due to a vow or fast during Ramadan, without good reason.
- Not fasting for that missed during the month of Ramadhan before the commencement of the next month of Ramadhan.
- To delay a prayer until its time is over.
- To discontinue an (ongoing) obligatory prayer.
- To abandon obligatory prayers.
- To abandon any other obligation.
- To delay performing Hajj from the year it becomes obligatory.
- Rejecting the orders of the scholars in their Shari'ah verdicts.
- Accepting payment for religious obligations that have to be carried out.

Jihad

- Not taking part in Jihad.
- Fleeing from battlefield.
- Selling arms to the disbelievers who wage war against the Muslims.

Qur'an

- Touching the holy Qur'an without formal purification, *Wudhu*.
- Selling the holy Qur'an.

Mosques

- Making the mosque unclean.

- Working to destroy mosques.
- Preventing people from going to mosques.
- Going to or staying in mosques while in a state of *Junub*.[18]
- The above individuals passing through the two grand mosques in Makkah and Medina.
- To disgrace the holy Ka'bah or other holy places.

The Believer

- Animosity towards believers.
- To defame a believer.
- To disgrace a believer.
- To hurt or abuse a believer.
- To threat or terrorise a believer.
- To make fun of the believers.
- To ridicule or demean the Muslims.
- To defame a believer in poetry etc.
- Abandoning the believers.

Others' Rights

- To publicise someone's secrets without his consent.
- Hoarding goods needed by the public.
- To falsely suspect others and act up on it.
- To falsely accuse people.
- Not to answer the Salaam greeting.
- Looking for others' shortcomings.
- Wounding or amputating limbs of someone's body.
- Beating someone for no reason.
- Detaining someone for no reason.

---

[18] An individual is in a state of *Junub* after sexual intercourse (or ejaculation), and therefore an obligatory *Ghusl* bathing is required to attain a spiritual purity as well as personal hygiene. Similarly a *Ghusl* bathing is also mandatory after the occurrence of menses or childbirth.

- Unlawful killing.
- Denying the rights of people that are due to them.
- Usurping the wealth or property of an orphan.
- Seizing and confiscating others' property, possession, or wealth.
- Reporting about individuals to oppressors.
- Confining a woman or young people for indecent acts.
- Obstructing the road of Muslims.

Male/Female Interaction

- Muslim woman not wearing Hijaab in public.
- For Muslim women to wear anything, in terms of cosmetics, perfume, clothing, etc. which would attract the attention of 'non-*Mahram*' men. [A 'non-*Mahram*' man is any man whom a woman must wear Hijaab from, and this ranges from friends to cousins and brothers- and sisters-in-law, etc.]
- 'Non-*Mahram*' man and woman kissing one another.
- Kissing a person with lust, except for spouses.
- Touching the body of non-*Mahrams*, male or female respectively.
- Touching others with lust, except one's spouse.
- Women shaking hands with 'non-*Mahram*' men (and vice versa).
- Looking at a non-*Mahram* woman (or man respectively) with lust.[19]
- Looking at boys (or girls) or *Mahram* relatives with lust.
- Going to mixed swimming pools.
- Going to schools that would lead one to corruption.
- Looking at the private parts of others, (except for the spouses).
- To reveal one's private parts in the presence of others.

---

[19] It is Haraam for a man to look at a Muslim woman who does not wear Hijaab, even when without lust.

- Adultery.
- Homosexuality.
- Lesbianism.
- Paedophilia
- Accusing someone of adultery or homosexuality.

Marriage

- Proposing marriage to a married woman or to a woman during the *Eddah* period (of four months after divorce or after becoming a widow).
- False marriage (e.g. forcing either of the two parties to marry, or the marriage of a Muslim and an atheist, *Kafir,* (excluding People of the Book, i.e. Jews and Christian.))
- To marry one's *Mahram* relatives, or relatives by marriage, or by breast-feeding.

{*Mahram* relatives, in the case of the male, are those such as his mother, sisters, nieces, and aunts. [In the case of the female, the *Mahram* relatives are her father, brothers, nephews, and uncles.] Marriage is not allowed between *Mahram* relatives and therefore a woman does not wear Hijaab from her *Mahram* relatives. Non-*Mahram* relatives are those such as cousins, brothers- or sisters-in-law, etc. and a woman must wear Hijaab from her non-*Mahram* relatives. Marriage is allowed between cousins. – Editor's note.}

Marital

- For a husband not to have sex with his wife for more than four months.
- Masturbation – it is allowed if it is done by the spouse, for example in foreplay.
- For a husband to have sex with his wife when she is going through her monthly menstruation period.
- For a woman to go out of the house without the knowledge or permission of her husband. (This excludes cases that are considered necessary.)
- For spouses to publicise each other's secrets.

Children

- Not disciplining one's children such that it would lead them astray.
- Beating one's children in excess of discipline.
- For children to disobey their parents.
- Relating a child to someone other than his natural father.

Personal Conducts

- Lying.
- Fraud.
- Cheating.
- Cheating in weighing and measuring.
- Deception.
- Treachery.
- Hypocrisy.
- Forging a will.
- Stealing and robbery.
- Going against one's vow.
- Breaking one's covenant.
- Backbiting or listening to it.
- Slander and defamation or listening to it.
- To be jealous and to act up on it.
- To be haughty.
- To be extravagant.
- To wear gold or silk (applicable to men only).
- To use gold and silver utensils even for decorating reasons.
- Not keeping oneself clean from urine and other unclean substances.
- Endangering one's own life.

Food & Drink

- Drinking intoxicating liquors.
- Eating animal flesh not slaughtered according to Islamic law, also consuming forbidden animals' flesh such as pork, etc. [Except in circumstances when one's life is dependent upon consuming such meat.]
- Eating forbidden parts of the animals such as testicles.
- Eating and drinking of the unclean or that which has become unclean.
- Eating mud or other prohibited things.

Social

- To hurt neighbours.
- Looking into the houses of neighbours without permission.
- Sitting at a table where alcohol is served.
- Prevention of good deeds and charitable works.
- Sitting with people who make innovations in religion.
- Reaching power by unlawful means (in accordance to Islamic law).
- Extracting confessions through torture.
- Playing chess.
- To work as a pimp.
- Spreading corruption on earth.
- To create commotion by setting individuals against one another.
- To praise one in his presence and abuse him in his absence.
- Exhumation of graves.
- Sitting with those who indulge in meaningless talks about the signs of Allah.
- Frolic and frivolity - to engage in useless activities, which are wasteful and distract from the remembrance and the path of Allah.

- To practice astrology or seek the help of astrologers. (to believe in and take action accordingly.)
- To subdue ghosts, *Jinns* and angles, etc. or seek the help of those who practice them (to harm others).
- Practicing black magic, witchcraft, or seek the help of those who practice them.
- Hypnotism (except for necessary medical requirements)

Sin

- To consent in sin.
- To publicise one's sins.
- To publicise indecency.
- To help others commit sin.
- To persist in committing minor sins.
- To order or encourage others to commit evil or sin.
- Considering ones sins not seriously as such that would lead to disregarding repentance.
- Promoting indecent acts.

Oppression

- Oppression and transgression.
- Helping an oppressor and condoning his actions.
- To become employees of the oppressors.
- Asking for judgment from an oppressor unnecessarily.

Gambling

- Betting or any form of gambling.
- Manufacturing tools of gambling instruments.
- Betting in ways other then those mentioned in the section of Islamic laws about archery and horse racing.
- Taking part in conventional horseracing, unless they meet all conditions approved by Shari'ah.

Music etc.
- Dancing.
- Singing and listening to it.
- Visiting nightclubs, discos, etc.
- Manufacturing, buying, selling, or using musical instruments.

Truth
- To accept or give bribe to hide a truth or make something false prevail.
- Presenting false testimony.
- Destruction of the truth.
- Swearing a false oath.
- Hiding a testimony.
- Hiding the truth.

Falsehood
- Accepting false religions, like Sufism, Baha'i, etc.
- To become a member of parties of falsehood like communism etc.
- Keeping, buying, selling, teaching and publicising false and misleading literature.
- The learning of corrupting subjects, or teaching them to other than those who want to refute them.

Miscellaneous
- Making statues, as well as buying, selling, and promoting them for the purpose of worship.
- Buying and selling of fighting dogs and swine.
- Taking and giving usury and brokerage about it.
- Shaving one's or others' beards.
- To be self-praising about one's own worships.
- A fury that leads to Haram.

- To break one's bond with relatives.
- Earning by unlawful things and means.
- To write erotic poetry about a chaste woman or a boy, etc.
- The use of intoxicants, whether drinking, selling, buying, farming, making, using its money, taking it from others, renting property for it, or using it in other ways like for dressing injuries unnecessarily.

Some of the conducts above may be related to others in the list, but they have been included for the seriousness of the conduct, as this has been indicated by various Qur'anic verses or Prophetic Hadiths or traditions.

It should be noted that some of the conducts mentioned above constitute *Kufr* (apostasy), some are *Shirk* (association), some are Major sins, and some are subject to *Kaffarah* (payment of fine or compensation), or subject to *Hadd* (punishment predefined in the Qur'an or the Hadith) or *Ta'zir* (punishment as prescribed by the judge). These are detailed in relevant jurisprudence texts.

(B) Unethical Conducts

The abominable habits and moral traits that should be avoided are many. The scholars of ethics have mentioned them in their books and here we shall mention most of them even though some of them, according to Shari'ah, are prohibited.

- To seek revenge.
- To boast about oneself.
- To be very optimistic about oneself.
- To consider one's own good deeds as great.
- To belittle other's good deeds.
- To consider other's bad deeds as great.
- To belittle one's own bad deeds.
- Not to care about one's own bad conduct and ignore other's protests against it.

- To look down up on people.
- To cause inconvenience to others.
- Hurting others even though an act causing it may not be unlawful, such as building one's house such that it blocks light or air from reaching the neighbour's.
- Insulting others even if not in unlawful ways.
- Frightening people even if not to the unlawful degrees.
- Hostility even if less than the unlawful limits.
- The use of bad words even if not unlawful.

- Jealousy.
- Wanting.
- To be rancorous and vindictive.
- To be stingy.
- To be malevolent.
- To be greedy.
- To be hasty.
- To cause commotion.
- To be hardhearted.
- To be awkward and not to get on with others.
- To be bad mannered.
- To be arrogant.
- To show off even in non-worship matters.
- To suspect people.
- To be afraid of people.
- Going back on one's promise.
- To be excessive in sexual lust.
- To have no self-respect.
- To have a low self-esteem and enthusiasm.
- To have no sense of honour.

- To have eager and fervour unnecessarily.

- Publicising matters that would have been better to be kept private.
- Lying when joking.
- To accuse someone of something in a joke.
- To make fun of others.
- To joke a lot.
- Too much laughing.

- To rely on others.
- To burden others.
- Doing useless things.
- Talking about things that are not one's concern.
- Spying on things that are not one's business.

- Taking good deeds lightly.
- Neglecting desirable acts.
- Persisting on detestable matters.
- To be curious about indecent things.
- Involving one self in undesirable matters, even if they are not unlawful.

- To confine oneself with material issues, e.g. clothing and housing, etc. in a similar way to those who lead an extravagant life.
- To express grief in hardship.
- To complain about life.
- To grief about worldly things.
- To have long worldly hopes.
- To be unhappy about one's possession in life.

- To be unconcerned about issues of the hereafter.
- Love of being praised.
- Love of leadership or high position.
- Love of this world.
- Love of wealth.
- To be too busy in earning.
- To be too wealthy that would lead to arrogance.

- To be pessimist about Allah.
- Not to have trust in Allah.
- To ignore Allah's guidance, and warnings, etc.
- Not to care about the rules of Shari'ah.

- Discrimination, fanaticism, and racism.
- To get angry without justifiable reasons.
- To be disrespectful to the elders.
- To be unkind to children.
- To be unfair.
- To be ungrateful.
- To be unthankful.
- To be two-faced.
- To be insolent.
- To neglect the believers.
- To sleep a lot.
- To have no work or skills.
- Not to observe cleanliness.
- Scrupulosity and obsession, even in worldly matters.
- To be either extremist in one's affairs or indifferent.
- Associating with sinners.
- Keeping company of contemptible individuals.

(C) Good Moral Conducts

- To have confidence in the promises of Allah.
- To belittle oneself before Allah.
- To spend for the cause of Allah.
- To take comfort with Allah.
- To repent from unlawful things that Allah dislikes.
- To submit oneself to the orders of Allah in all matters.
- To have trust in Allah.
- To love Allah and those whom He has ordered to love.
- To love because of Allah.
- To dislike because of Allah.
- To have fear of Allah.
- To have hope in Allah.
- To be deliberate in one's affairs.
- To have fairness.
- To be independent of people.
- Altruism or selflessness.
- To help people.
- To train oneself in good matters.
- To encourage others to do good deeds.
- To stop others from doing abominable things.
- To bring reform among people.
- To be sincere in one's deeds.
- To be good to one's parents.
- To be humble.
- To visit friends.
- To be friendly.
- To be steadfast in good deeds.
- To be forbearing.
- To be good mannered.

- To protect the rights of the neighbours.
- To be concerned about one's sins (both past and possible future ones.)
- Not to have all hopes in deeds.
- To be considerate with people.
- Not to do or practice anything (spiritually or materially) to the extent that it results in extreme pressure on oneself.
- To be nice with the family and children.
- To be content with destiny.
- To forsake worldly pleasures.
- To be respectful.
- To be protective of people.
- To correct one's mistakes.
- To be pleasant in one's speech with others.
- To be thankful of the bounties.
- To reform people with good language.
- To spent much in charity and help the weak.
- To maintain good relations with one's relatives.
- To spread peace and harmony.
- To reach-out for the weak, sick and the orphans.
- To be clean.
- Not to publicise people's shortcomings.
- To be the same in out side and in side in all matters.
- To be truthful and stay away from lies even in joking.
- To have patience.
- To be hospitable to guests.
- To accept invitations.
- To give and accept gifts on traditional occasions.
- To forgive people.
- To be chaste.
- To have justice in all matters.

- To have reverence for religious people.
- To stay away from despicable individuals.
- To have courage.
- To love the poor.
- To strife against one's desires.
- To give loans.
- To help the believers in need.
- To prevent any harm from reaching the believers.
- To keep a secret and not to publicises it.
- To mention people with good names.
- To hurry in doing good deeds.
- To bring one's self into account.
- To give good advise to believers.
- To intend to do good things.
- To cleanse one's soul and remove believers' shortcomings from it.
- To be pious.
- To be God fearing.
- To avoid doubtful matters (i.e. whether they are Halal or haram).
- To persevere with avoiding sin.
- To persevere on worship and prayers.
- Remembrance of death and the hereafter.
- To be content.
- To be bashful.
- To have a happy face.

The Author

Ayatollah al-Udhma Imam Muhammad Shirazi is the Religious Authority, or *Marje'*, to millions of Muslims around the globe. A charismatic leader who is known for his high moral values, modesty and spirituality, Imam Shirazi is a mentor and a source of aspiration to Muslims; and the means of access to authentic knowledge and teachings of Islam. He has tirelessly devoted himself, and his life, to the affairs of Muslims in particular, and to that of mankind in general. He has made extensive contributions in various fields of learning ranging from Jurisprudence and Theology to Politics, Economics, Law, Sociology and Human Rights.

Imam Muhammad Shirazi was born in the holy city of Najaf, Iraq, in 1347 AH (Muslim calendar), 1927 AD. He settled in the holy city of Karbala, Iraq, at the age of nine, alongside his father. After primary education, the young Shirazi continued his studies in different branches of learning under his father's guidance as well as those of various other eminent scholars and specialists. In the course of his training he showed a remarkable talent and appetite for learning as well as a tireless commitment to his work and the cause he believed in. His extraordinary ability, and effort, earned him the recognition, by his father and other *Marje's* and scholars, of being a *Mujtahid*; a qualified religious scholar in the sciences of Islamic jurisprudence and law. He was subsequently able to assume the office of the Marje' at the early age of 33 in 1960. His followers are found in many countries around the globe.

Imam Shirazi is distinguished for his intellectual ability and holistic vision. He has written various specialized studies that are considered to be among the most important references in the Islamic sciences of beliefs or doctrine, ethics, politics, economics, sociology, law, human rights, etc. He has enriched the world with his staggering contribution of more than 1000 books, treatise and studies on various branches of learning. His works range from simple introductory books for the young generations to literary and scientific masterpieces. Deeply rooted in the holy Qur'an and the Teachings of the Prophet of Islam, his vision and theories cover areas such as Politics, Economics, Government, Management, Sociology, Theology, Philosophy, History and Islamic Law. His work on Islamic Jurisprudence (*al-Fiqh* series) for example constitutes 150 volumes, which run into more than 70,000 pages. Through his original thoughts and ideas he has championed the causes of issues such as the family, human right, freedom of expression, political pluralism, non-violence, and Shura or consultative system of leadership.

Imam Shirazi believes in the fundamental and elementary nature of freedom in mankind. He calls for freedom of expression, political plurality, debate and discussion, tolerance and forgiveness. He strongly believes in the consultative system of leadership and calls for the establishment of the leadership council of religious authorities. He calls for the establishment of the universal Islamic government to encompass all the Muslim countries. These and other ideas are discussed in detail in his books.

o-o-o-o-O-o-o-o-o

Teachings of Islam

A site dedicated to the cause of Islam, Muslims and Mankind.

Islam aims to bring about prosperity to all mankind. One of the leading authorities on Islam today, Imam Muhammad Shirazi, calls upon all Muslims to adhere to the teachings of Islam in all domains in order to regain their former glory and the salvation of mankind. These teachings include:

- PEACE in every aspect.
- NON-VIOLENCE in all conducts.
- FREEDOM of expression, belief, etc.
- PLURALISM of political parties.
- CONSULTATIVE System of Leadership.
- The re-creation of the single Muslim nation - without geographical borders, passports between them, as stated by Allah:

  "This, your community is a single community and I am your Lord; so worship Me."

- The revival of Islamic brotherhood throughout this nation:

  "The believers are brothers."

- Freedom from all the man-made laws, shackles and restrictions as stated in the Qur'an:

  "... and (the Prophet Muhammad (S)) releases them from their heavy burdens and from the shackles that were upon them."

This is the official website of Imam Shirazi. You can email your queries on issues of concern to the site at: queries@shirazi.org.uk

Other Publications by *fountain books*

1. Aspects of the Political Theory of Imam Muhammad Shirazi

Muhammad G. Ayub is a well-known Islamist political activist within the Iraqi circle who has established a long history of political struggle behind him. He was attracted by the views of the Imam Muhammad Shirazi in the fields of social and political sciences. This prompted the author to write this book to introduce the reader to these views that have remained relatively unknown to the Muslim activists and reformists. It covers such aspects on politics as freedom of expression, party-political pluralism and organisation, social justice, peace and non-violence, human rights, consultation system of government, etc.

2. Islamic System of Government

In this introductory book the author outlines the basic principles of a government based on the teachings of Islam. The author begins with the aim and objectives of the government according to Islam and the extent of its authority. He then addresses, from the Islamic viewpoint, the significance and fundamental nature of such issues as consultative system of government, judicial system, freedoms, party political pluralism, social justice, human rights, foreign policy, etc. The author also outlines the policies of a government on issues such as education, welfare, health, crime, services, etc. as well as such matters as the government's income, and authority.

3. If Islam Were To Be Established

This book can serve as the Muslim's guide to the Islamic government. If an Islamist opposition group has a plan for an Islamic government, this book would help to check various aspects of the plan. In the absence of such a plan, this book would present one. To the non-Muslims, the book presents a glimpse of a typical Islamic system of government. The book would also serve as a yardstick for anyone to check the practices of any government that claims to have implemented an Islamic system of government.

4. The Family

In this book the author highlights the problems he sees primarily in Islamic societies and particularly in the west today, from the phenomenon of unmarried young men and women through to birth control and contraception. He surveys the idea of marriage in various religions and schools of thought and discusses polygamy from the Islamic perspective. As well as being a call to the Muslim world to revert to the true teachings of Islam, this book can also be of use as an introduction to others who seek some answers to the social problems of today. This is because Islam has detailed teachings, which promise success in every area of human life on individual and societal levels, and what's more their practicality has been historically proven.

5. The Qur'an: When was it compiled?

In this book the author addresses the issues of when the Holy Qur'an was compiled, on what and whose instructions was this task carried out and who accomplished its compilation in the form that it is available today. In this work the author presents undisputable evidence as to address these crucial questions. Through historical, methodical and logical analyses, the author establishes how and when the compilation of the Holy Qur'an was achieved. In the latter half of the book the author cites many Prophetic traditions on the significance of the learning and recitation of Holy Qur'an. It is a must read for every Muslim, and any non-Muslim who follows Islamic issues.

6. War, Peace and Non-violence: An Islamic perspective

In this work the author addresses three controversial issues, which have come to be associated with Islam. Through his extensive knowledge of the teachings of Islam, the author presents the Islamic stand on war, peace and non-violence, as found in the traditions and teachings of the Prophet of Islam, which could serve as exemplary models for Mankind. Detailed accounts of the traditions of Prophet in his dealings with his foes during war or peace times are presented in this book, which gives the reader a clear insight into the way and the basis upon which the Prophet of Islam used to conduct his affairs in this respect.

Also available from:

- www.ebooks.com
- www.amazon.co.uk

<u>Europe</u>

- *Alif International*,
  109 Kings Avenue,
  Watford,
  Herts. WD1 7SB,
  UK
  Tel. + 44 1923 240 844
  Fax + 44 1923 237 722.

<u>USA</u>

- *TTQ, Inc.*
  P.O. Box 731115
  Elmhurst, New York 11373
  USA
  Tel. + 1 718 446 6472
  Fax + 1 718 446 4370

Free Muslim is an independent, humanitarian and political, Islamic organisation that strives to encourage and promote the policies of non-violence to be upheld and practiced by everyone and in all aspects of life.

Free Muslim aims to defend the values and teachings of Islam, to educate the Muslim society with the spirit of debate and respecting the opinions of others in searching for the truth.

The objectives of Free Muslim is to promote and crystallise non-violence in accordance with Islamic law, to intermediate between the nations and organisations and their Muslim governments and conciliate between them in order to safeguard the Muslim community and eliminate any traces of violence, to call for the freedom of prisoners of conscience, to call for the abrogation of the Death penalty in accordance with Islamic law, to promote and present the teachings of Islam accurately and to correct the false attributes which are made to Islam by the mass media, to promote the just peace and implement social justice throughout the world, according to the teaching of Islam.

Free Muslim
PO Box 13/5570
Beirut, Lebanon
www.freemuslim.org
freemuslim@freemuslim.org
Tel: 00 9611 275 675
Fax: 00 9611 541 483
Fax: 00 114 134 871 747 (USA)